SALVATORE FERRAGAMO

INSPIRATION AND VISION

edited by Stefania Ricci, Sergio Risaliti

SKIRA

Graphic Project
Studio Contri Toscano

Editing
Cinzia Morisco

Translations
Lucian Comoy, Christopher
Evans, Marco Migotto,
Leslie Ray for Language
Consulting Congressi, Milan
Steve Chaplin

First published in Italy in 2011
by Skira Editore S.p.A.
Palazzo Casati Stampa
via Torino 61
20123 Milano
Italy
www.skira.net

Printed and bound in Italy.
First edition

ISBN: 978-88-572-1133-6

Distributed in USA, Canada,
Central & South America
by Rizzoli International
Publications, Inc., 300 Park
Avenue South, New York, NY
10010, USA.
Distributed elsewhere in the
world by Thames and Hudson
Ltd., 181A High Holborn,
London WC1V 7QX, United
Kingdom.

Cover
Sonia Delaunay, illustrations
for the book *La prose du
Transsibérien et de la petite
Jehanne de France (Prose of
Trans-Siberian and of Little
Jehanne of France)* by Blaise
Cendrars, 1913. Florence,
Biblioteca Nazionale Centrale

SALVATORE FERRAGAMO
INSPIRATION AND VISION

Florence
Salvatore Ferragamo
Museum
Palazzo Spini Feroni
May 27th 2011 –
March 12th 2012

Under the Patronage of
Comune di Firenze

Exhibition promoted
and organised by
Salvatore Ferragamo
Museum

Catalogue edited by
Stefania Ricci
Sergio Risaliti

with the collaboration of
Stephen Jones

Graphic Project
Studio Contri Toscano

Photography
Antonio Quattrone

Exhibition curated by
Stefania Ricci
Sergio Risaliti

with the collaboration of
Stephen Jones

Organisational
Secretariat
Francesca Piani
Laura Buonocore

Layout Design
Silvia Cilembrini
Fabio Leoncini

Video Research
and Project
Daniele Tommaso

The exhibition curators
and authors of the catalogue
wish to thank

Ministero per i Beni e le
Attività Culturali
Soprintendenza per i Beni
Architettonici, Paesaggistici,
Storici, Artistici ed
Etnoantropologici per
le province di Firenze, Pistoia
e Prato
Soprintendenza Speciale per
il Patrimonio Storico, Artistico
ed Etnoantropologico
e per il Polo Museale
della Città di Firenze
Soprintendenza per i
Beni Storici, Artistici ed
Etnoantropologici per le
province di Venezia, Belluno,
Padova e Treviso

Archivio Centrale dello Stato,
Rome
Biblioteca Nazionale Centrale
di Firenze
'Gaio Cilnio Mecenate'
National Archaeological
Museum, Arezzo
Musée des Tissus de Lyon,
France
Museo Civico L. Bailo,
Treviso
Musei Provinciali di Gorizia
National Archaeological
Museum, Florence
Natural History Museum,
Anthropology and Ethnology
Section and "La Specola",
Zoology Section, Florence
Stibbert Museum, Florence

Renzo Arbore Collection,
Rome
Biagiotti Cigna Foundation,
Rome
Marta Bindi Grassi
Collection, Florence
CLM Seeber Collection,
Rome

Farsettiarte, Prato
Stephen Jones Millinery
Archive, London
Sandro Michahelles
Collection, Florence
Ottavio and Rosita Missoni
Collection, Milan
Claudio Monnini Collection,
Milan
Private Collection, Florence
Private Collection, Lucca
Private Collection, Rome
Luigino Rossi Private
Collection, Venice
Museo Richard-Ginori della
Manifattura di Doccia, Sesto
Fiorentino (Florence)
The Bata Shoe Museum,
Toronto, Canada
Tornabuoni Arte, Florence

In particular, we wish
to thank

Cristina Acidini, Antonio
Addari, Paolo Agnelli,
Giuseppe Anichini, Renzo
Arbore, Kirsten Aschengreen
Piacenti, Agostino
Attanasio, Filippo Bacci di
Capaci, Fausto Barbagli,
Mariarosaria Barbera, Sonja
Bata, Martina Becattini,
Laura Biagiotti, Lavinia
Biagiotti Cigna, Marta Bindi
Grassi, Alexandra Biondi,
Chiara Boracchi, Mario
Bracciali, Laura Brazzini,
Isabel Bretones, Susan
Brown, Marco Brusamolin,
Antonella Cacciani, Roberto
Casamonti, Chiara Casolo
Ginelli, Filippo Ceccolini,
Lucia Chimirri, Giuseppina
Carlotta Cianferoni, Sofia
Ciucchi, Francesco Civita,
Massimiliano Colacicchi,
Marcello Contrucci,
Simona De Marco, Daniela
De Palma, Cornelia
de Uphaugh, Patrizia
Diani, Alvise di Canossa,
Maximilien Durand,
Garbine Eguia, Maria Eisl,
Carlo Esposito, Elisabetta
Farioli, Franco Farsetti,
Frediano Farsetti, Leonardo
Farsetti, Stefano Farsetti,
Stefano Frasconi, Simone
Frosecchi, Alessandro
Gazzotti, Cristina Gnoni,
Paola Goldoni, Philippe
Grillot, Marie-Hélène
Guelton, Paola Gusella,
Cristina Intelisano, Stephen
Jones, Dorothée Lécrivain,
Emanuele Lepri, Antonella
Maggiorelli, Alessandra
Marino, Alessandra Martina,
Audrey Mathieu, Marta
Mazza, Suzanne Mclean,
Sandro Michahelles,

Ottavio Missoni, Rosita
Missoni, Claire Morel,
Barbara Mucci, Carlo Nesi,
Rosella Nesi, Marco Pagni,
Cristina Panigada, Silvia
Petrioli, Daniela Porro,
Giovanni Pratesi, Elvira
Rainone, Lesley Robeson,
Giacomo Romano, Maria
Gloria Roselli, Luciano
Rosi Belliere, Federica
Rossi, Luigino Rossi, Oliva
Rucellai, Chiara Sainati,
Massimo Sanzani, Marie
Schoefer, Maria Letizia
Sebastiani, Elisabetta
Seeber Michahelles,
Raffaella Sgubin, Laura
Sini, Sebastiano Soldi,
Mara Spaggiari, Chiara
Stefani, Edoardo Testori,
Andrea Tremolada, Barbara
Vernocchi, Silvia Vilucchi,
Margherita Viola, Marco
Voena, Monica Zavattaro,
Alessandro Zuri

Special thanks to
Stefano Salvatici for having
contributed to the planning
of the section dedicated to
Stephen Jones and his hats.

Exhibition sponsors

CONTENTS

'We are all flowing with the eternal tide, and of the eternal tide only is there no end' SALVATORE FERRAGAMO

INTRODUCTION

STEFANIA RICCI

Does an artist always have a source of inspiration in developing a creative idea? Is it only a single, easily identifiable source or is it a number of things which are distant in time and space, mixed as in a cocktail and beyond the confines of knowledge? How does inspiration interact with an individual's personal history, culture, talent, technical experience, and emotions? How is it possible that multiple impressions lead to similar ideas produced analogously by different minds over the same span of time?

These many questions are the basis of this exhibition and were continuously asked as we travelled back in time through Salvatore Ferragamo's imagination; it was a journey in search of the sources of his creativity which over more than forty years of work produced countless models for footwear and four-hundred patents. In such an analysis, much can be taken into consideration, as is the case for every respected artist, but there are always key stages. In Ferragamo's case, we concentrated on two periods in his life where conditions encouraged inspiration and visions to flourish and which influenced the artist's later life: his move to California around 1915 and his return to Florence in 1927, which in the Twenties was the artistic and cultural heart of Italy.

Salvatore Ferragamo's experience in Hollywood, surrounded by the emerging cinematographic industry, led to the young Italian's fame and success as 'Shoemaker to the Stars,' but it was also an opportunity to meet extraordinary people, study endlessly and experiment. The discovery in 1922 of the funereal treasures of the Pharaoh Tutankhamon in Egypt—to mention only one well-known example greatly influencing the world of fashion generally—had a strong creative impact on film. Ferragamo quickly maximised the potential of this in the models and decoration of sandals which Cecil B. DeMille—the great silent film director who was fascinated by the Orient—ordered Salvatore to make for the lead actors of the film, *The Ten Commandments*. This was repeated a few years later when the Villa dei Misteri in Pompeii was discovered and became an inspiration to contemporary art and graphics; Salvatore took inspiration and created a line of shoes called *Pompeian*, and the *Coturno* sandal, which was laced at the ankle like a Roman sandal and hence evoked the classical world. It became the preferred image on the shoemaker's early advertising.

The Californian world and the culture of the territory were sources of continue inspiration for Ferragamo. Decoration on accessories and clothes used by the American Indians, the combination of fabrics and colours of quilts made by Quaker communities, the richness of South American craftsmanship using the most extravagant materials, such as multicoloured bird feathers, are reflected in the models of those years and return decades later in his innovations like a signature style.

Ferragamo's decision to return to Italy in 1927 and stay in Florence came from the need to find the skills to produce hand-made shoes, and a desire to find authentic sources of inspiration in the local artisan and artistic culture. In Florence Ferragamo was impressed not only by the architecture so famous to international tourism, but also by the many public and private city collections which held extraordinary examples of the applied arts, to which Ferragamo by nature was attracted. Frederick Stibbert's eclectic and tasteful collection, for example, influenced Ferragamo in the shape of his shoes, the weaving of the upper soles, the design of embroideries, which was faithfully reproduced from clothes in the collection. Similar sensations were produced by the National Archaelogical Museum and the Natural History Museum, which were limitless wellsprings of ideas, intuitions, and creative experiments, in the past as much as in the present.

Alongside an interest in tradition and historical finds, Ferragamo was also affected by experiments with material and colour carried out during that time by avant-garde artists, the Futurists in particular, for whom in the Twenties Florence itself was a first order cultural epicentre.

Ferragamo's innate ability to assimilate the spirit of the times continued throughout his life; this can be seen in influences and analogies with contemporary artists and designers who achieved aesthetic and technological outcomes similar to Ferragamo's but in different fields. For example, Jacobsen created his famous egg armchair the same year Ferragamo patented the leather 'shell-shaped sole,' a transposition in shoe form of the armchair's ergonomics, and Andy Warhol designed shoes in gold leaf in 1956, the same time Ferragamo created his sandal in 18-carat gold for the wife of a rich magnate. In his autobiography Ferragamo writes, 'How else can I explain my sense of design? I do not have to search for styles. When I need new ones, I select from those that present themselves to my mind, as I select an apple from the laden dish upon my table.'[1] With these words the creative Ferragamo seems to negate any inspiration or reference to what does not come from within. In another part of his autobiography he speaks more clearly about reminiscence and reincarnation, on the one hand re-echoing theosophical theories in vogue in certain Florentine circles of the Twenties and Thirties,

as suggested by Sergio Risaliti and Luca Scarlini in this catalogue, but also for the obvious difficulty of explaining creativity in words. In reality creativity cannot be defined, it can only be identified.

The topic is fascinating and complex, it is complex as reconstructing the approach that leads to the birth of certain flashes of inspiration which are at the root of everything and that intertwine with technical skill, personal culture, curiosity, intuitive ability and courage. In Ferragamo's case there are an almost infinite number of directions to take. The work of rebuilding some of the impressions that led to the creation of artisan products unique to the history of fashion, means omitting thousands of others that would have the same validity and weight. All of us who worked on this project are aware of this and we apologise if on looking the exhibition there is a feeling that certain details are missing and that key exemplars have been ignored. For this reason we wanted to end the show with a section dedicated to a contemporary creative artist, Stephen Jones, who works in fashion and with accessories, as Ferragamo did, but with hats and not shoes. The first time we met Stephen Jones was in Antwerp on the occasion of an exhibition of his work. From that moment several points of similarity with Salvatore Ferragamo's work emerged which justified his inclusion in this exhibition. Jones' creations are collector's items, as are Salvatore's shoes. There is a strong artisanship component requiring technical mastery and knowledge, and that is typical of haute couture. Jones' pieces demonstrate passion and obsessive and constant experimentation with several materials—often used for the first time in hats, as it was the case in Salvatore Ferragamo's shoes—and a great sensitivity to the world of art. Every day he wrestles with creativity in the creation of his hats, which are more works of art than accessories to wear, and so close to Ferragamo's models they seem inspired by them.

We asked Stephen Jones the same questions that obsessed us throughout this project: what is inspiration for an artist, what creativity really is, whether or not there are favourable conditions from which creative thoughts spring, and whether this is the result of creative DNA or there is a formula for becoming creative over time. Perhaps we can connect the subtle thread that brings together inspiration, intuition and new concept that is its final product only through the words of those who on a daily basis grapple with the nonstop creation of something new.

[1] S. Ferragamo, *Shoemaker of Dreams* (original edition London: George G. Harray & Co. Ltd, 1957, Livorno: Sillabe, 2006), p. 59.

etruscan abstractions

Etruscan Art, *Olla*, 7th century BC, pasted ceramic painted with geometrical pattern from Poggio Buco (GR), Florence, National Archaeological Museum

Salvatore Ferragamo, *Court shoe*, 1958–59, kid upper, Florence, Salvatore Ferragamo Museum

sandals or cothurni

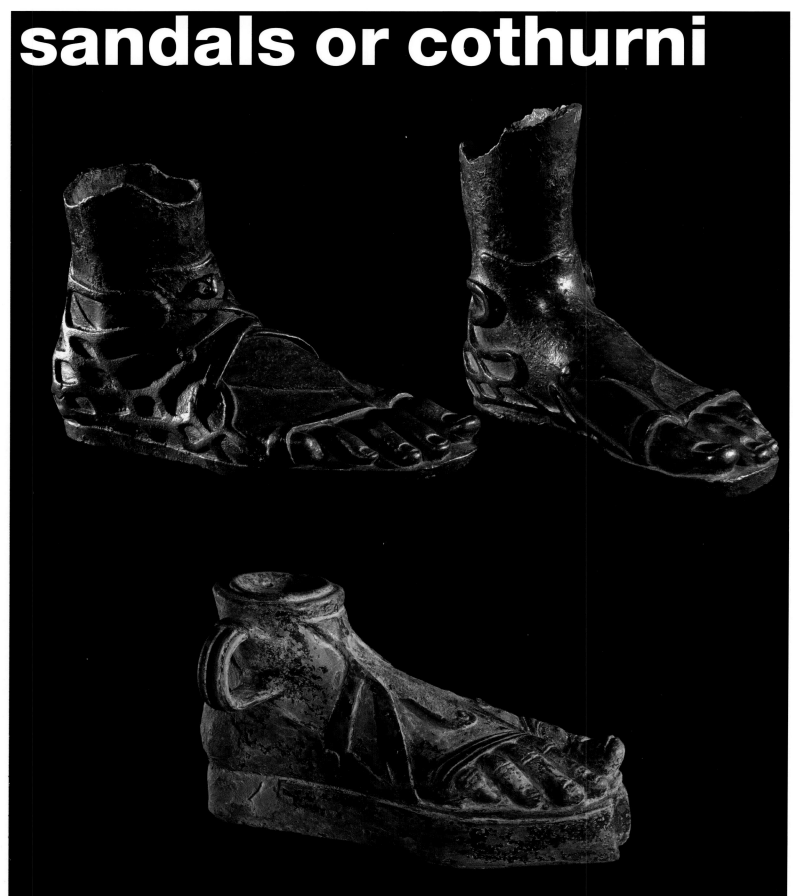

Roman Art, *Couple of foot with statue fit*, imperial age, 1st–3rd century AD, bronze. Florence, National Archaeological Museum

Hellenistic Art, *Askos*, 3rd century BC, ceramic and black paint. Florence, National Archaeological Museum

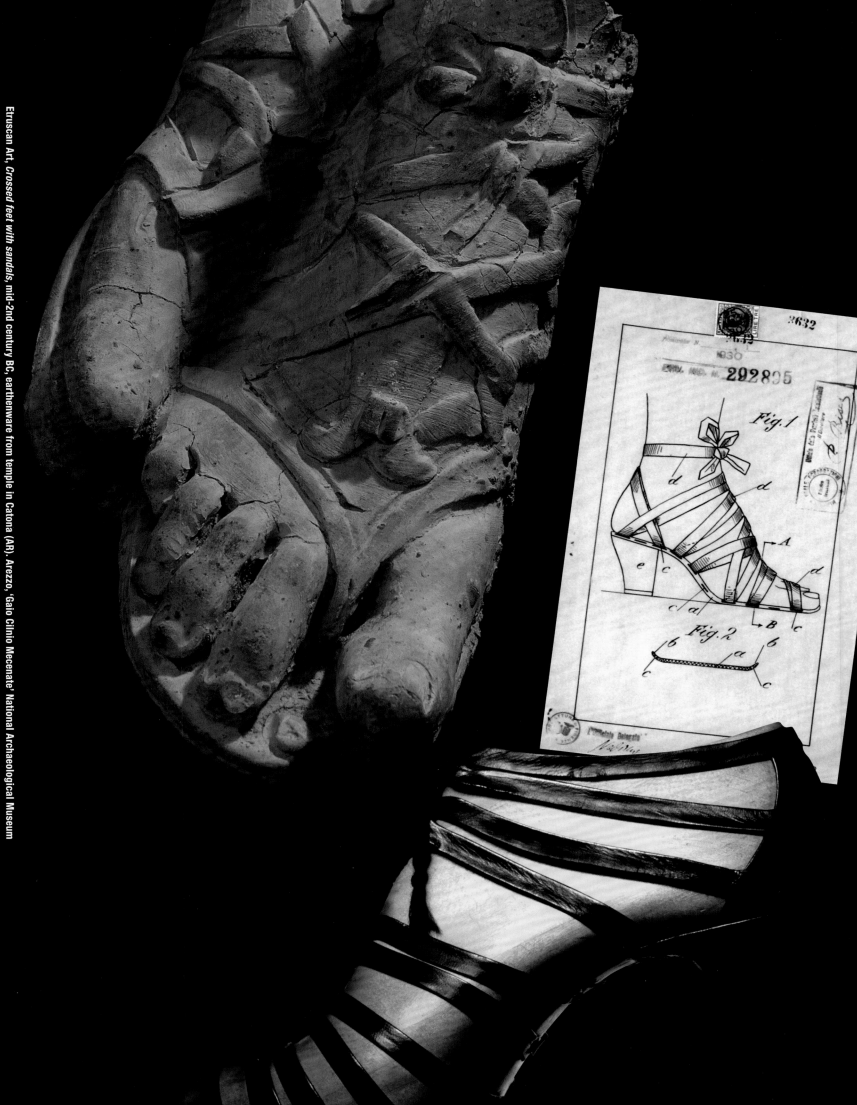

Etruscan Art, *Crossed feet with sandals*, mid-2nd century BC, earthenware from temple in Catona (AR), Arezzo, 'Gaio Clinio Mecenate' National Archaeological Museum

Salvatore Ferragamo, *Sandal system with a means of tying ribbons or the like so as to wrap the foot as desired*, patent no. 292895, February 4th 1932. Rome, Archivio Centrale dello Stato

Salvatore Ferragamo, *Sandal*, 1930, kid upper. Florence, Salvatore Ferragamo Museum

wedges and platforms

Northern Italian manufacture, *Women's slippers*, second half of the 16th century, round-toed slippers with high arched wooden support, covered with leather and decorated with braids and fringes in silk. Florence, Stibbert Museum

Salvatore Ferragamo, *Sandal*, 1939–40, velvet and kid upper, wood heel and 'flat through' sole covered with kid, cork platform insole covered with kid. Florence, Salvatore Ferragamo Museum

Italian manufacture, *Women's shoe (incomplete)*, around 1640, elongated toe, squared at the top, upper in leather decorated with braids that form a zigzag pattern. Florence, Stibbert Museum

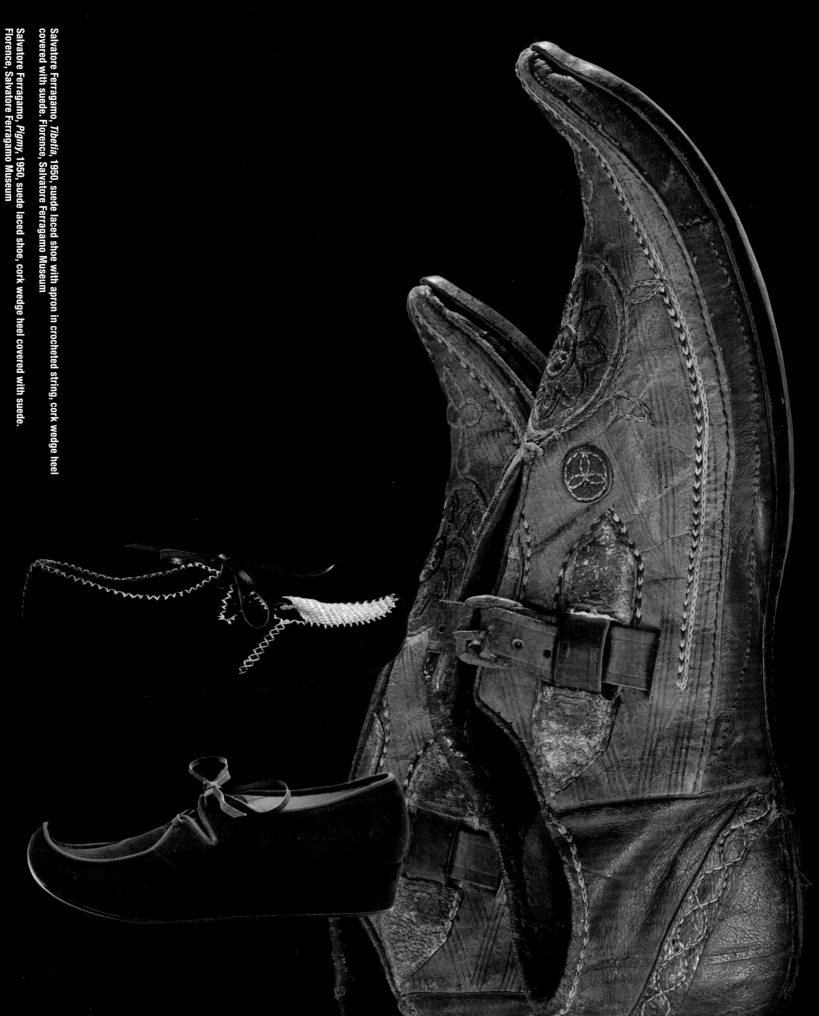

Salvatore Ferragamo, *Tibetia*, 1950, suede laced shoe with apron in crocheted string, cork wedge heel covered with suede. Florence, Salvatore Ferragamo Museum

Salvatore Ferragamo, *Pigmy*, 1950, suede laced shoe, cork wedge heel covered with suede. Florence, Salvatore Ferragamo Museum

Caucasian manufacture, *Men's shoes*, 19th century, upper in leather stamped with a striped pattern, quarters and finishings in leather, long and curved toe. Florence, Stibbert Museum

Chinese manufacture, *Woman's Jacket*, Ching dynasty, 19th century, embroidered silk with a flounce, silk collar and cuffs, Manchu style embroidered flowers, birds and butterflies. Florence, Stibbert Museum

Salvatore Ferragamo, *Sandal*, 1938, kid upper, cork platform sole covered with painted satin in floral motifs. Florence, Salvatore Ferragamo Museum

manchu style

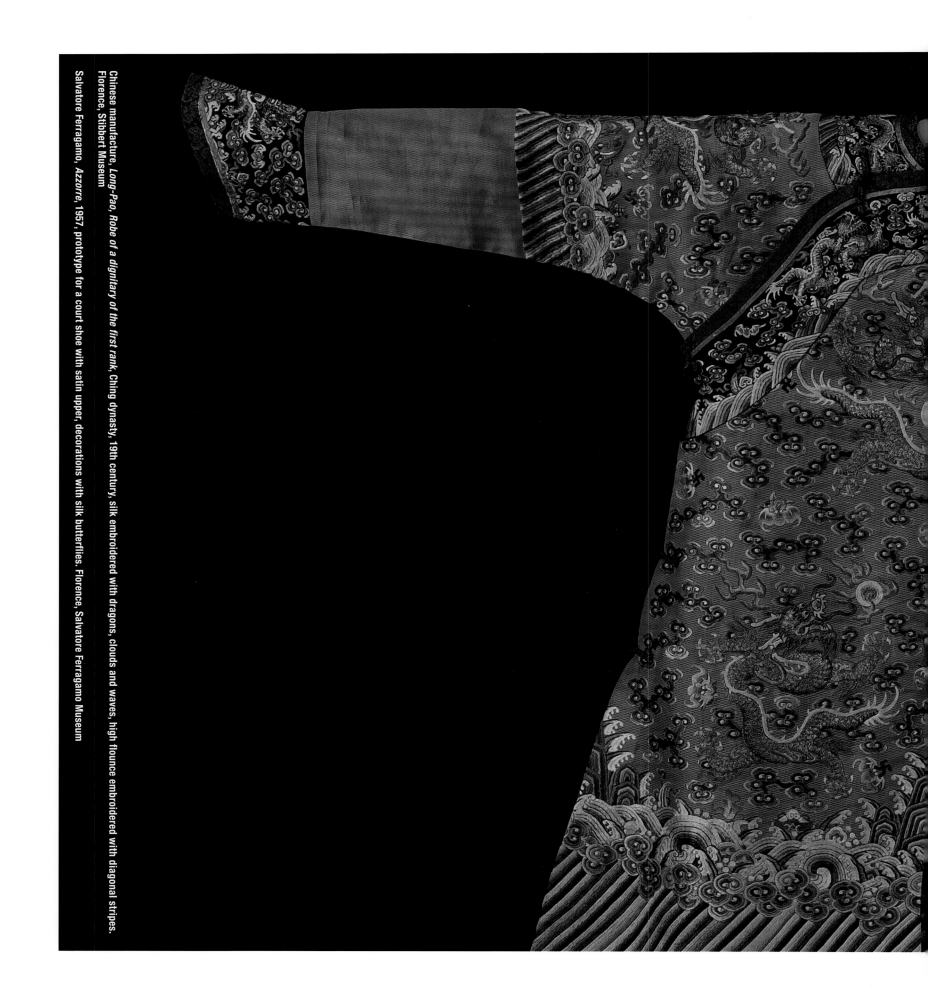

Chinese manufacture, *Long-Pao, Robe of a dignitary of the first rank*, Ching dynasty, 19th century, silk embroidered with dragons, clouds and waves, high flounce embroidered with diagonal stripes. Florence, Stibbert Museum

Salvatore Ferragamo, *Azzorre*, 1957, prototype for a court shoe with satin upper, decorations with silk butterflies. Florence, Salvatore Ferragamo Museum

ching dynasty

the indian bride

Indian manufacture, *Maharata figure of bride*, 18th century, wedding dress composed of veil, tulle bodice with gold stitching, sash of tulle embroidered with flowers around the waist, skirt with embroidered flounce and trousers. Florence, Stibbert Museum

Salvatore Ferragamo, *Liu*, 1950, satin mule embroidered with floral motifs with internal cork wedge heel. Florence, Salvatore Ferragamo Museum

samurai

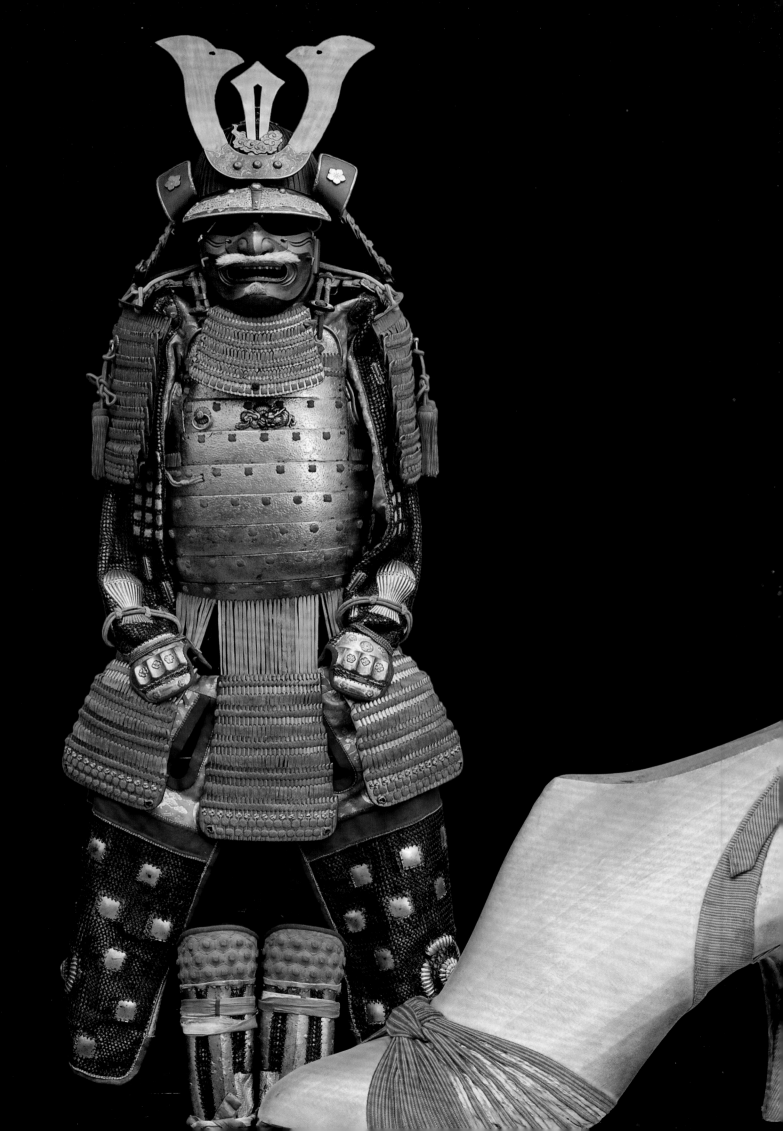

Japanese manufacture, *Japanese Armour, Akaito odoshi niimai-do tosei gusoku,* third quarter of the 16th century; the corset dates from a few years later; the rest of the suit is from the Edo period. Armour of a high-ranking samurai of the Hosokawa clan, characterised by connections made of silk tape. The helmet is signed by Myochin Fusamune. Florence, Stibbert Museum

Salvatore Ferragamo, *Sapo,* 1956–57, prototype for a sandal in silk, cellophane and grosgrain. Florence, Salvatore Ferragamo Museum

saho

Beni-Amer Girls, Assaorta plateau (Eritrea) 'Missione Eritrea' Collection, 1905–06. Florence, Historical Photographic Archives of the Natural History Museum, Anthropology and Ethnology Section

Salvatore Ferragamo, Sandal, 1955, multicoloured patchwork raffia upper. Florence, Salvatore Ferragamo Museum

Saho manufacture (Eritrea), *Handbag*, 19th century, cotton canvas, shells and glass beads. Florence, Natural History Museum, Anthropology and Ethnology Section

Saho manufacture (Eritrea), *Handbag*, 19th century, leather, shells, glass beads. Florence, Natural History Museum, Anthropology and Ethnology Section

Salvatore Ferragamo, *Fiesta*, 1957, prototype for a sandal in kid decorated with Venetian glass beads. Florence, Salvatore Ferragamo Museum

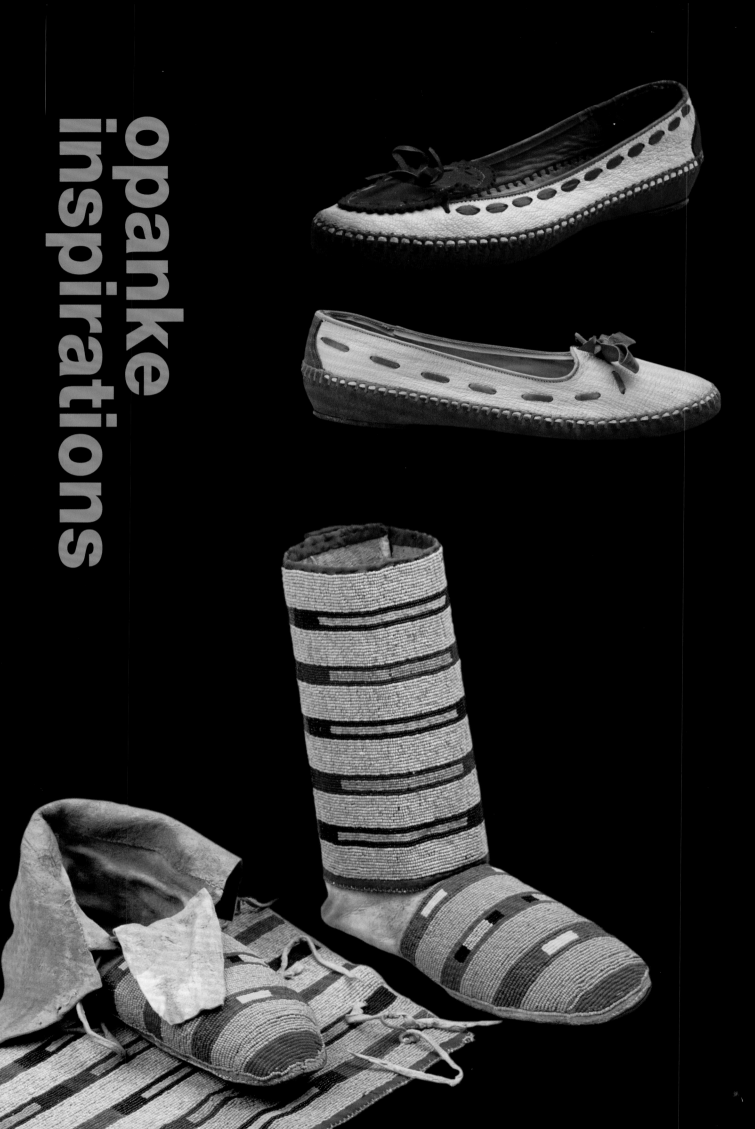

opanke inspirations

Salvatore Ferragamo, *Ballerina*, 1953–57, kid upper, back and vamp in suede and kid, low leather heel, opanke suede sole, 'Ballerina by Ferragamo' line. Florence, Salvatore Ferragamo Museum

Salvatore Ferragamo, *Ballerina*, 1953–57, kid upper, low leather heel, opanke sole and suede back, 'Ballerina by Ferragamo' line. Florence, Salvatore Ferragamo Museum

Nez Perce manufacture (North America), *Pair of moccasins*, 1930, beaded upper, tanned skin with matching beaded leggings. Toronto, Bata Shoe Museum

Freckled Face, Arapahoe, Great Plains (USA), photo F.A. Rinehart, 1899. Florence, Historical Photographic Archives of the Natural History Museum, Anthropology and Ethnology Section

Sioux manufacture (North America), *Pair of moccasins*, 1890, quelled and beaded moccasins in tanned skin. Toronto, Bata Shoe Museum

gran chaco

Chamacoco manufacture (Gran Chaco, Bolivia), *Feathers diadem*, 19th century, feathers, plumes, vegetable fibres. Florence, Natural History Museum, Anthropology and Ethnology Section

Salvatore Ferragamo, *Variopinta*, 1957, prototype for a sandal in bird's feathers and kid. Florence, Salvatore Ferragamo Museum

Chamacoco manufacture (Gran Chaco, Bolivia), *Feathers sceptres*, 19th century, feathers, plumes, vegetable fibres, wood, rattlesnake's tail. Florence, Natural History Museum, Anthropology and Ethnology Section

Mbayá Caduveo Indian of the Nabileque River with traditional tattoos, Gran Chaco, South America, photo by G. Boggiani, print of 1904. Florence, Historical Photographic Archives of the Natural History Museum, Anthropology and Ethnology Section

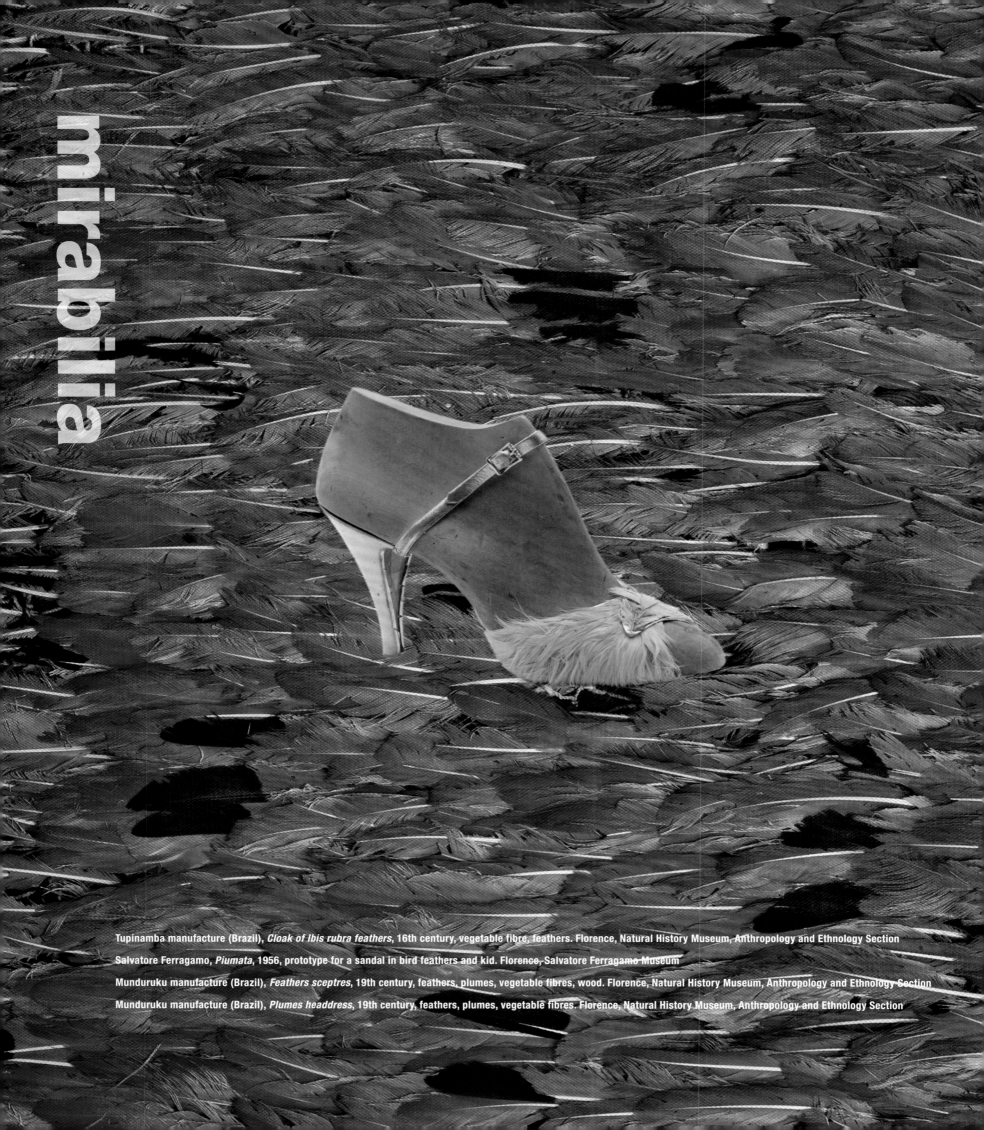

mirabilia

Tupinamba manufacture (Brazil), *Cloak of Ibis rubra feathers*, 16th century, vegetable fibre, feathers. Florence, Natural History Museum, Anthropology and Ethnology Section

Salvatore Ferragamo, *Piumata*, 1956, prototype for a sandal in bird feathers and kid. Florence, Salvatore Ferragamo Museum

Munduruku manufacture (Brazil), *Feathers sceptres*, 19th century, feathers, plumes, vegetable fibres, wood. Florence, Natural History Museum, Anthropology and Ethnology Section

Munduruku manufacture (Brazil), *Plumes headdress*, 19th century, feathers, plumes, vegetable fibres. Florence, Natural History Museum, Anthropology and Ethnology Section

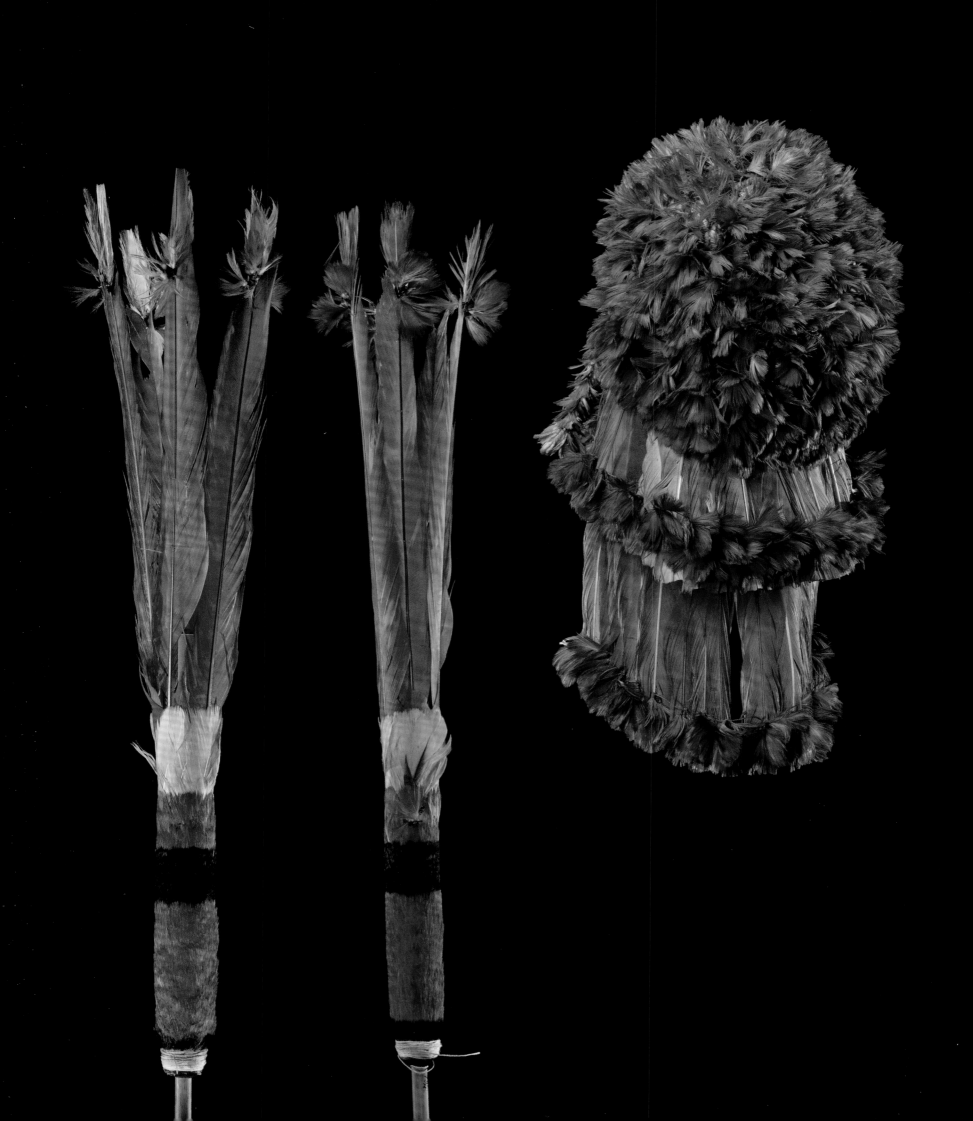

paradisea

Lophorina superba, naturalised specimen. Florence, Natural History Museum, 'La Specola' Zoology Section

Salvatore Ferragamo, *Chantal*, 1961, prototype for a court shoe in satin with silver, rhinestones and ornamental feathers. Florence, Salvatore Ferragamo Museum

Paradisea raggiana, naturalised specimen. Florence, Natural History Museum, 'La Specola' Zoology Section

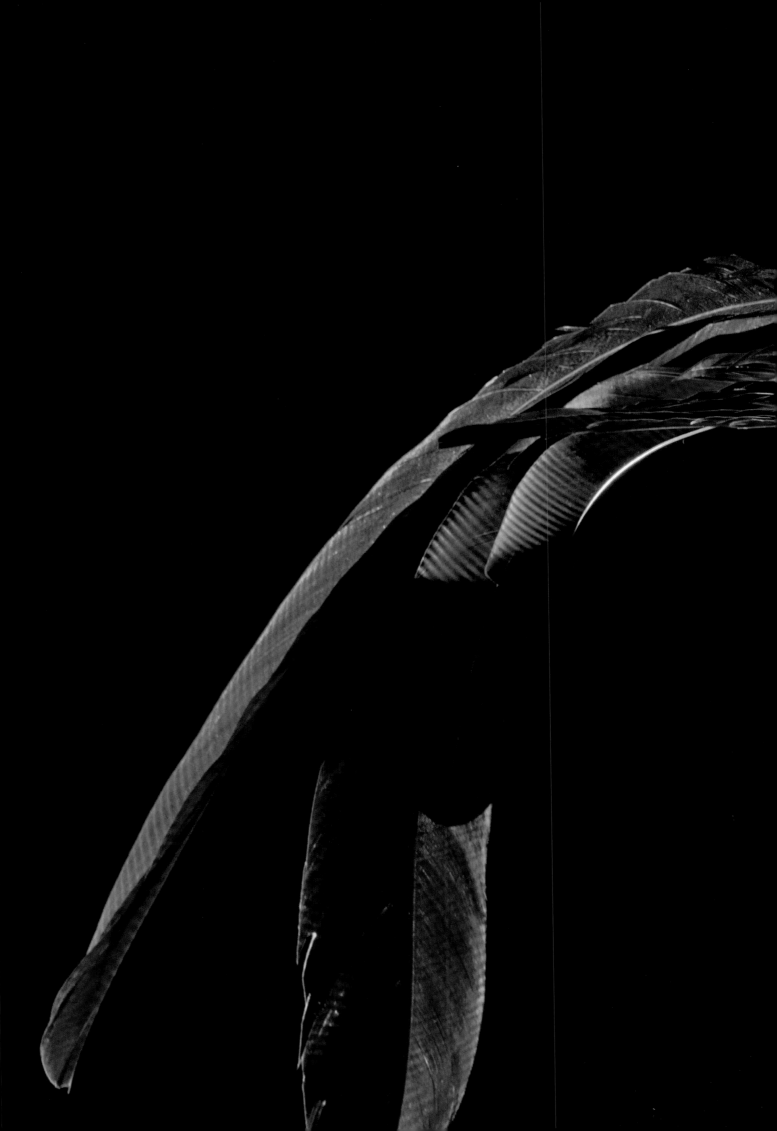

ars

Astrapia nigra, naturalised specimen. Florence, Natural History Museum, 'La Specola' Zoology Section

Salvatore Ferragamo, *Ars*, 1957–60, prototype for a high-heeled sandal in satin painted with birds of paradise motif. Florence, Salvatore Ferragamo Museum

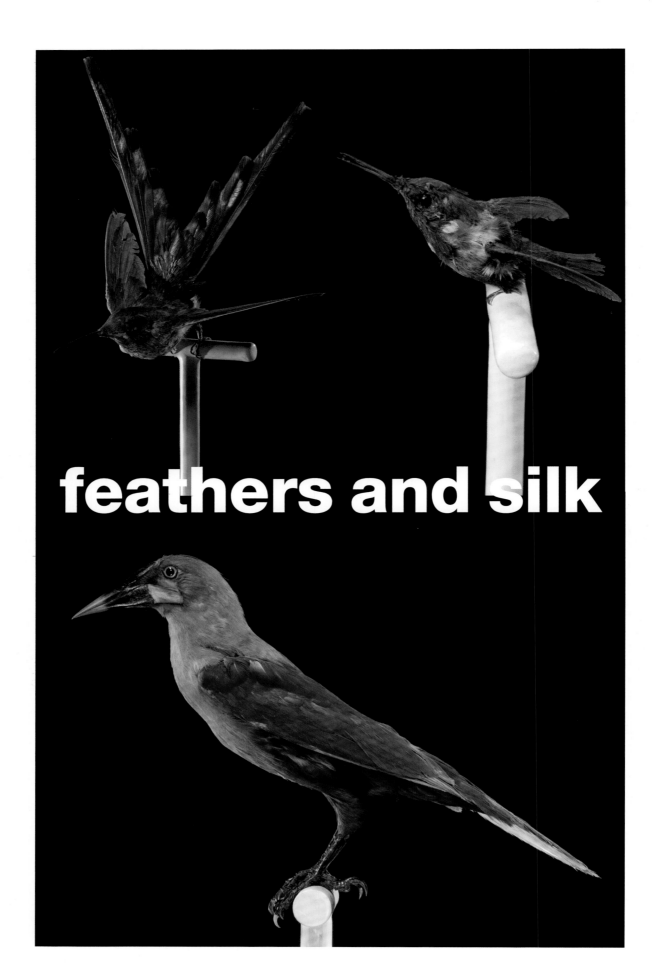

feathers and silk

Sappho sparganura, naturalised specimen. Florence, Natural History Museum, 'La Specola' Zoology Section

Chaetocercus heliodor, naturalised specimen. Florence, Natural History Museum, 'La Specola' Zoology Section

Psarocolius yuracares, naturalised specimen. Florence, Natural History Museum, 'La Specola' Zoology Section

Coracias garrulus, naturalised specimen. Florence, Natural History Museum, 'La Specola' Zoology Section

Salvatore Ferragamo, *Chantal*, 1961, prototype for a court shoe in satin with silver, rhinestones and ornamental feathers. Florence, Salvatore Ferragamo Museum

nature in colour

Naturalised specimens. Florence, Natural History Museum, 'La Specola' Zoology Section

Salvatore Ferragamo, *Prototypes for a court shoe*, satin with silver, rhinestones and ornamental feathers. Florence, Salvatore Ferragamo Museum

Rupicola peruviana

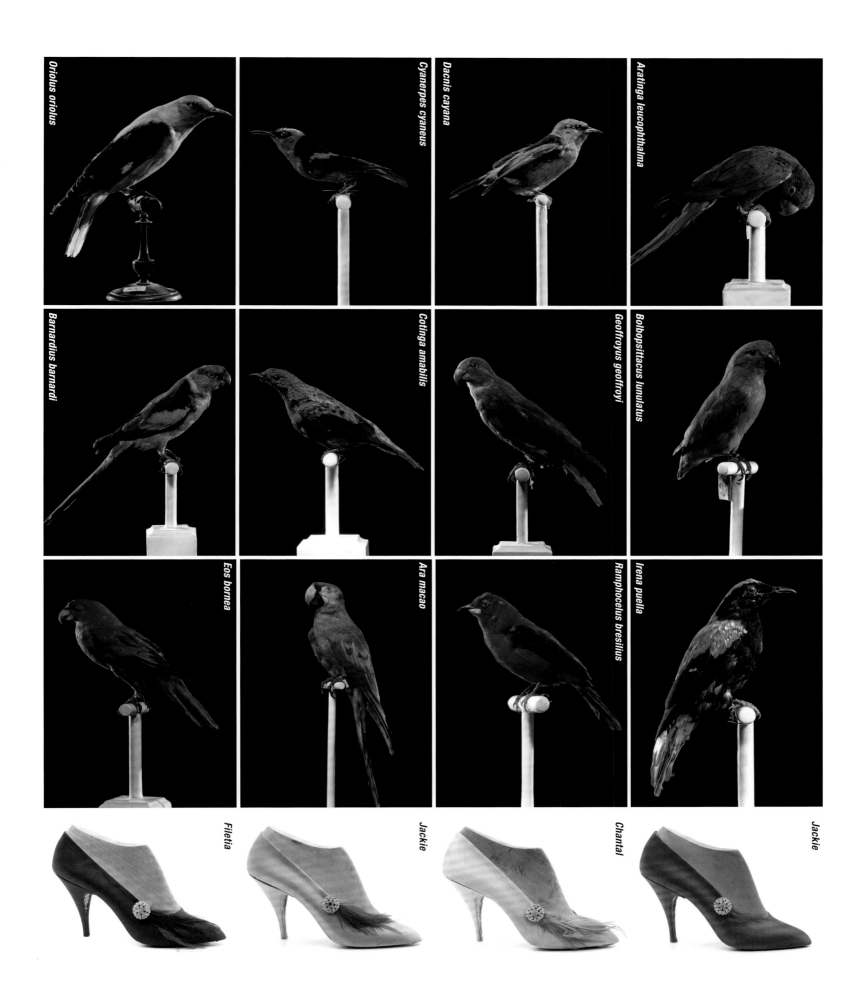

Oriolus oriolus

Cyanerpes cyaneus

Dacnis cayana

Aratinga leucophthalma

Barnardius barnardi

Cotinga amabilis

Geoffroyus geoffroyi

Bolbopsittacus lunulatus

Eos bornea

Ara macao

Ramphocelus bresilius

Irena puella

Filetia

Jackie

Chantal

Jackie

in the shape of a rhinoceros horn

'A true researcher never grows old; every eternal drive lies outside the sphere of a lifetime and the more the external shell falls apart the clearer, more resplendent and powerful becomes the core' NOVALIS

REMINISCENCE AND INSPIRATION IN SALVATORE FERRAGAMO

SERGIO RISALITI

1 | REMINISCENCE

THE MEMORY RETURNING

Many claim that inspiration is associated with the continuous development of images that the world and history unfold before our eyes. Others believe that those who are inspired receive ideas from superior entities. In the latter case inspiration and imagination would depend on a kind of celestial fertilisation. In the *Divine Comedy* (*Purgatory* XVII, 25) Dante says: 'Next shower'd into my fantasy.' For Italo Calvino, who tackles the issue in his *Six Memos for the Next Millennium*, 'Dante is meditating on images that formed directly in his mind, depicting classical and biblical examples of wrath chastised; he realizes that these images rain down from the heavens—that is, God sends them to him.'[1] Inspiration is supposedly therefore a gift from heaven, something that falls like rain on the artist's head to fertilise neurons. In contrast with modern science, much more inclined to explain the transmission of culture by means of genetics,[2] an ancient school of thought explains inspiration in the *artifex*—whether artist or artisan—with metempsychosis. Otherwise, how do we explain the fertility of inventions in a single individual, the relations that suddenly emerge between one sign and another, between images far removed in time and space, the particular predisposition of an individual in a given artistic sphere or in a handicraft activity? According to this philosophy, talent, when it is innate, is supposedly the cyclical manifestation of the higher qualities of an individual soul that finds itself attaining perfection from life to life, from rebirth to rebirth. In this regard, René Guénon applies a clearcut distinction between professional learning and initiation in a trade (in Italian 'mestiere,' from the Latin *ministerium*).[3] In the profane and modern conception, 'a man can devote himself to any profession, and also change it at will, as though this profession were something purely external to him, without any real bond with what he truly is, that is, with what makes him himself and not another.'[4] In the traditional conception, on the contrary, 'each person must normally perform the function for which he is destined through his very nature, with the aptitudes that this essentially implies; and he cannot perform another, without this involving a serious disorder, which will have repercussions on the entire social organization of which he is part; worse still, if a disorder of this kind becomes general, its effects will have a consequence on the cosmic sphere itself, as all things

are linked together by rigorous correspondences.'[5] In this case, writes Guénon, it is 'the essential qualities of human beings that determine their activities;'[6] in the mechanicistic dimension, on the other hand, 'these qualities do not count, and individuals are not considered as anything but interchangeable and purely numerical units.'[7] Consequently, in a 'sacred' and 'ritual' vision of works and the arts, a substantial difference exists between teaching by initiation—that is, traditional—and profane teaching. So, what is learned from outside during childhood or in the professional life of an adult is not essential, 'whatever the quantity of the notions' accumulated is. It is quite another thing 'to reawaken the latent possibilities that the human being carries within himself (and this, after all, is the true meaning of "Platonic reminiscence").'[8] Therefore knowledge must be appraised in qualitative and not quantitative terms (even if we wish to define this as inspiration), because it is a 'memory returning,'[9] a flashback of lives lived in other bodies, the recognition of experiences already had (including the contemplation of the world of Ideas). In this sense the familiarisation with trade-*ministerium* of the talented youngster (whether an artist or an artisan, a painter or a shoemaker) always occurs through an initiation. It is more or less a matter of reawakening the latent possibilities that lie in the depths of the self, as though they were almost a golden reserve to be spent with each rebirth.

We cannot know if and when Ferragamo read the texts of Plato,[10] yet in his autobiography we discover that he is well informed on the theory of reminiscence: 'Nor have I had to learn in the accepted sense. From my first

'Today, now that I can reflect and ponder,' Ferragamo writes in his autobiography, 'I have come to a belief in the reincarnation of Man in his evolution towards perfection. It seems to me that though my ideas are born out of the past, yet they reach me perfected. They come to me full-blown on the cosmic tide, all ancient errors smoothed away.'

days with shoes—yes, even with the little white shoes I made for my sisters—I have remembered all about shoemaking. I have remembered: that is the only way to describe it. I have only to sit down and think, and the answer comes to me out off the memory of days—it can be only this—when in some previous existence upon this earth I was a shoemaker.'[11] At another point in the story, the artisan-artist is even more precise and makes reference to a search for perfection in the broader framework of human evolution, which within that conception would not finish during the course of a single life: 'Today, now that I can reflect and ponder, I have come to a belief in the reincarnation of Man in his evolution towards perfection. It seems to me that though my ideas are born out of the past, yet they reach me perfected. They come to me full-blown on the cosmic tide, all ancient errors smoothed away. I remember vividly my first experience of this "memory returning".'[12] Note how in this passage Ferragamo associates reflection with meditation, in other words, a level of understanding that is more spiritual than philosophical, an understanding that transcends the analytical dimension of rational thought, to tackle, through the emptying of the self, a cognitive experience based on transcendental vision, on the profound revelation of the nature of being.

More than once, the 'Shoemaker to the Stars' returns to the theme of metempsychosis. He talks of it with simplicity and purity, and is always sure of what he says. On the last page of his life story, Ferragamo presents us with 'secret truths clearly exposed:'[13] 'I have only just begun to work'—he says—'I am still perfecting myself for the work I have to do in the future, the work to which I have been called. I have plenty of time. I know I am going to do it. If it is not done with this body, it will be done with another.'[14] Thus, in line with the 'traditional conception of the trade,' according to which everyone must perform the function for which they are destined and cannot perform any other, since all the things are tied together by 'rigorous correspondences,'[15] we feel we can say that Ferragamo recognised these mysterious connections in his destiny: 'I was born to be a shoemaker. I know it; I have always known it. As I look back now on the long lesson of my life I can see quite clearly how strong, how remorseless, how unrelenting is the passion within me that has driven me on and on, along a path strewn with so many hardships. Many were the times when I wondered why I was not as other men, why I was not like my elder brothers, content with the things they possessed, hankering not after the fruits of tomorrow. Yet I could not swerve from my pretestined path, no matter what the cost. It was against Nature. It was against God.'[16]

THE SECRET MODULE

Ferragamo has always identified himself in the cobbler's trade, and many times he has defended the artistic qualities of craftsmanship, setting them against the results achieved with machines.[17] For this reason he has always been spoken of as an artisan-artist and not as a stylist. But, in his case, the artisan is the *artifex*: according to that tradition, which does not distinguish between artist and artisan, major and minor arts, when the activity respects metaphysical principles not conditioned by a succession of tastes and fashions. To explain better, we will again have recourse to Guénon, who writes: 'For the ancients the *artifex* is, without distinction, a man who conducts an art or a craft; but, in reality, he is neither an artist nor an artisan in today's meaning of those words (the word "artisan" tends to be increasingly disappearing from contemporary language); he is something more than both, because, at least originally, his activity was associated with principles of a much more profound order.'[18] To build perfect, made-to-measure shoes: this was Ferragamo's dream; he wanted to lighten the weight of the body, covering and lifting the feet with mathematical precision. The relations within the forms to be worn on the feet were studied by him snatching the secrets from nature, 'the supreme architect from whom Man has borrowed and adapted so many of his ideas.'[19] To do this, he necessarily had to respect the golden section that governs the establishing of proportions and harmonious relationships between the parts in play, the basis of every architectural construction, of music and of anatomy. So he will have made his own the concepts of *modulus* and *ordinatio*, as in Vitruvius and in Leon Battista Alberti, also learned unconsciously, walking the streets of Florence, the city so loved by him for the beauty and harmony of its churches and buildings. At one point in his autobiography, he meditates on the philosophy of opposites: when he must find the optimum solution to give elasticity to the shoe, while respecting the dynamics of movement, of the counterposing of weights and forces, of the involvement of the limbs.[20] We have the impression that he has studied the relationship between the physical structure of man and that of the cosmos, that he thinks of his shoes as organic forms on scientific bases. He perfected his talent, *de facto*, with studies of anatomy and chemistry and rejected mass production of a mechanical type, having as his main aim that of creating footwear made-to-measure, according to the canons of craftsmanship-art. He wanted to cure, almost coming into contact with the intimate personality of every one of his clients through the study of the feet,[21] which he touched like a shaman, recognising the person's mood: 'What do I mean when I say that feet talk to me? Just that: they communicate the character of the person. Let a nervous

woman place her foot, perfectly relaxed, into my hand, and I know at once that she is nervous because a current, powerful as a small electric shock, passes through her foot to my palm. I feel the reaction as clearly as I feel the sun when it is warm and the wind when it blows cold. The degree of nervousness I can tell you by the degree of shock: the more powerful it is, the more nervy is the person. When there is no shock I can tell you at once that the person is without temper, without nerves.'[22] Ferragamo was therefore thinking of the repetition of a *module* rather than the mechanical reproduction of models. A *module* defined on the basis of harmonious studies to be applied perfectly to the anatomical structure of individual feet, all the same and all different. Having grasped the secret of creating the perfect shoe, his obsession became the arch of the foot. Then came the plumb line, the correspondence between the organs of the body and the foot, between the latter and psychic health; in a word, man in his completeness, built according to the principle of eurhythmics. In this sense we can talk of development and improvement of a module for an ideal shoe from which to depart and to which to refer for every new and more personal manufacture, rather than of production of models or types to be produced in series with the timescales and the speed of machines and mass commerce.

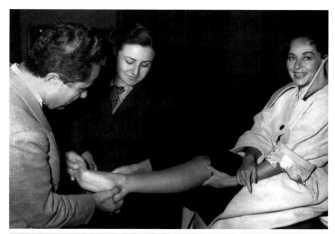

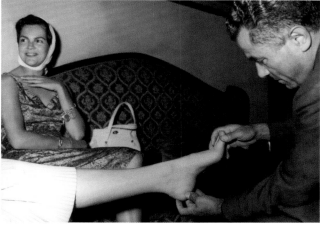

Ferragamo touching the feet recognised people's mood. Salvatore Ferragamo with Paulette Goddard (1954) and with Gabriella di Savoia (1958)

THE GOLDEN NUMBER

We have spoken of archetypes, of golden section, of correspondences among architecture, music and anatomy. In the 20th century the study of the golden section, of Pythagoreanism and of Neoplatonic geometry returned to fashion with Gino Severini (Cortona 1883 – Paris 1966) who in *Dal cubismo al classicismo* (1921)[23] meditated on an art of harmony built on the knowledge of the unchangeable laws of number: 'In the golden ages of art the philosophers were geometrists and artists were first geometrists and then philosophers.'[24] Or: 'Art must develop in contact with Science: these two expressions of man are inseparable from each other, and both are inseparable from that unique and religious principle that is the origin of Everything.'[25] And again: 'The work of art must be *eurhythmic*. That is, *all* its elements must

be composed in a whole, according to a constant relationship that obeys certain laws [...]. This aesthetics based on number relates back to the laws with which we have interpreted and explained the universe, starting from Pythagoras and Plato. They have taught us that everything in creation has a rhythm according to the laws of number, and only with these laws can we recreate, reconstruct, an equivalent of equilibrium and universal harmony. The purpose of art can be defined in this way: to reconstruct the universe according to the very laws that govern it.'[26] In that text, full of references to the ancient and of humanistic citations, Severini deals with proportions and 'the golden number that is encountered when tackling the problem of the golden section.'[27] He is convinced that 'all the creations of the ancient art *obeyed the fixed laws of number,* that *nothing was entrusted to chance or was only result of the taste*, and that even the smallest details always depended on a unitary measurement, that is, on a *module*.'[28] He then explains the difference between empiricism and the study of absolute laws, stigmatises the fetishism of originality at all costs, the separation between Art and Science, explains the distance that separates creation based on instinct from that based on reason. Then he warns artists of the risk they run when they base their own work on instinctive reflexes that place 'the painter on the same plane as a hairdresser or a milliner.'[29] Severini offers this example: 'Indeed, how does a milliner obtain a balanced hat? If he puts a ribbon on the right he will put an equivalent one on the left; if the ribbon is too large, he will cut off a piece and he will add something to the equivalent on the left, and so on until he has achieved the balance that his taste suggests to him. There are highly skilled milliners, who have a very refined taste for balance between shapes and colours, but this does not mean they have artistic and constructive inclinations.'[30] At a certain point, Severini praises the figure of the triangle and cites in this regard that of ancient Egypt 'famous for the beauty of his ratios, which enabled the Egyptians to build temples, cathedrals and ancient statues in all the great periods of art;'[31] he then goes on to explain to his readers that this triangle, used for measuring land, was also used 'by the Indians and by the Chinese, who talk of it in the *Tcheou-Pei*, the sacred book of calculation'[32] always with a religious and sacred meaning. Finally he reminds us that in '*Isis and Osiris* Plutarch defines it as the most beautiful triangle: "And we have reason to believe that the Egyptians compared the nature of the universe with the most beautiful triangle of all, that to which Plato probably also referred, in the *Republic*, in terms of nuptial figure: that triangle in which the side that forms the right angle is equal to *three*, the base is equal to *four* and the third line, the so-called subtended (the hypotenuse), is equal to *five*.

Ferragamo based his work on the combination between aesthetics and anatomy, his studies on the feet led to the definition of a module for an ideal shoe from which to depart, rather than mass production. At the same time as Ferragamo, some artists of the 20th century such as Gino Severini considered that Art must develop with Science and base their aesthetics on respect for numerical laws. Gino Severini, *Rythme de danse à l'opéra (Dancing rhythm at the opera)*, 1950 Oil on canvas, 131 x 161.5 cm Prato, Farsettiarte Collection

The latter has the same power as the other two that form the right angle, so the perpendicular can be compared to the male, the base to the female, and the subtended what arises from the two".'[33]

Suggestions of symbols and names of divinities, again connected to geometry and numbers (the triangle and the golden number, Isis and Osiris), came back into current events with the archaeological campaigns launched in the Valley of the Kings by the eccentric Theodore Davis in 1902, and then with the discovery of the tomb of Tutankhamon by Howard Carter in 1922, with the subsequent discovery of the sarcophagus, the mummy of the pharaoh and his famous golden mask, engraved on the rear of which are prayers from the *Book of the Dead* and references to Osiris. News and legends accompanied by highly evocative images were circulated all over the world by the media of that time, and it is possible that they also encouraged meditations on Egyptian culture on the part of Salvatore Ferragamo, perhaps prompting him to create a series of golden shoes, with heels in the shape of an inverted pyramid-ziggurat. Shoes oriented in a Pythagorean sense, coloured in the metaphysical and solar gold of that ancient religion. Sand-coloured shoes, conceived as hieroglyphs and religious formulas. While in California, in front of the movie cameras, pyramids and sphinxes, temples and obelisks were raised, making the inhabitants of that arcane world, so filled with mysteries and magic, come to life again.

2 | INITIATION

'A child perched on a chair staring with eyes wide open at the hands of the cobbler working on shoes.'
Salvatore Ferragamo

THE TEN COMMANDMENTS

Stampalia was the steamboat on which Ferragamo travelled heading for America. For that trip Salvatore bought himself a new coat with a rabbit fur collar and an umbrella. A citizen's attire. New York appeared as a dizzy forest of skyscrapers, high as mountains. A dream. In Boston, the youngster rejoined his sisters Clotilde and Alessandrina; but his destiny was elsewhere. In California his brothers Alfonso, Girolamo and Secondino awaited him. Deserts, Rocky Mountains, grasslands; after a trip lasting six days and six nights, Santa Barbara welcomed him with its sun. Looking through the car window, he admired the beautiful villas and gardens in flower. Salvatore, abounding with talent, immediately became famous. The difference between his shoes, made with top-level Italian craftsmanship-art, and others, entirely machine made, was enormous. A short time later, Ferragamo designed footwear to fit the feet of the stars of cinema. Legendary names: 'Lottie Pickford, effervescent, excitable and extravagant, the antithesis of her sister [...]. Afterwards came the Costello sisters, Barbara La Marr, Helen Hayward, Pola Negri, Mae McAvoy,' and among the men Douglas Fairbanks. But it was with the transfer of his 'firm' to Hollywood that success arrived. Ferragamo was to join the circle of the major production houses, working with directors of the calibre of Cecil B. DeMille, D. W. Griffith and James Cruze. He designed and modelled shoes for the feet of Rudolph Valentino, John Barrymore, Theda Bara and John Gilbert; even for the supple ballerinas of the Grauman's Egyptian Theatre. It was a prolific period, abounding in new styles, in successful insights. He created bizarre shoes, tried out shapes and combinations of increasingly unusual materials: 'The corkscrew heels, studded with imitation pearls, for Gloria Swanson; the multicoloured satin slippers for Lillian Gish; the rainbow-coloured evening shoes with ankle straps and tall gold heels for Dolores Del Rio; and the *Serpent* shoes for Esther Ralston. These were a pair of black and gold slippers with a spike heel.'[34] A shoe embellished with the head of a real snake whose 'sleek, flexible bodies, with golden scales painted as life-like as I could make them, writhed half-way up her beautiful legs.'[35]
In Santa Barbara he experienced the 'memory returning' for the first time, when the film studio gave him 'the task

Some moments from the discovery of the tomb of the pharaoh Tutankhamon with its furnishings by archaeologist Howard Carter in 1922

Following the discovery of the tomb of Tutankhamon, Ferragamo created footwear in an Egyptian style for the protagonists of the film by Cecil B. DeMille, *The Ten Commandments*

Coinciding with archaeological discoveries underway in the Valley of the Kings by Theodore Davis in 1902 and then by Howard Carter with the discovery of the tomb of Tutankhamon and his precious funerary equipment in the early Twenties, great influence was exercised by the culture of Ancient Egypt in the world of art and fashion. In these images the clothes for the ballet *Cleopatra* by the company De Basil designed in 1917 by Sonia and Robert Delaunay, and Claudette Colbert as DeMille's *Cleopatra* in 1934 testify to the lasting fascination of the myth of Ancient Egypt in the world of movies and fashion

of designing beautiful shoes to accompany beautiful dresses for costume and historical films.' Ferragamo, observing the actors' clothes, understood that he lacked the historical and necessary notions in creating shoes that were correct from the stylistic point of view. So he rushed to the library and consulted fashion books: 'I flicked the pages, looking at the plates, examining the styles of the dresses of the Fifteenth century, the Sixteenth, the frivolity of the Seventeenth, the severity of the Eighteenth, and so on down to the Nineteenth century. When I closed the book all its knowledge belonged to me. I knew what I could do with my shoes and I knew what I should do. I also knew how to make the styles differently, their ancient clumsiness smoothed, their inadequacies remedied by the application of new thoughts, new designs, new materials, I do not mean that I studied the footwear in the book: there were few examples shown, because it is a subject sadly neglected by the historians of fashion. I studied the costumes and knew how to harmonize my shoe design with those dresses.'[36] It was therefore not the quantity of information added that saved Ferragamo at that time, but a series of stimuli that awakened latent possibilities in him. In Hollywood a second episode of reminiscence occurred. Salvatore was invited to present some models of footwear to Cecil B. DeMille, who was already a living legend then, and obviously before that very important meeting he was extremely agitated: '*The Ten Commandments*'—writes Ferragamo—'presented me with a problem similar to the one I had solved in Santa Barbara when I was first asked to provide shoes for a costume film. It was my first commission for a shoe wardrobe of a spectacle film of such immensity, and it staggered me. I had never designed shoes for the Babylonian-Egyptian-Hebraic period, and my knowledge of the time was nil. On an inspiration I sat down and designed a high-fronted shoe with a mask reaching

half-way up the shinbone, and on the mask I placed the heads of beasts–lions and leopards and strange mythical creatures. For the Egyptian I designed an open half-shoe with sandal effect. When the girl I now employed to turn my rough pencil sketches into detailed instructions had completed the work, I took the results to DeMille. [...] He was delighted and enthusiastic. He had no corrections to make, but I had—or thought I had. To satisfy my curiosity I went to the local library and scanned every book I could find which might give me a clue to the closeness of my imagined ideas to the actual footwear of the real Mosaic period. I found virtually nothing. [...] I was thus unable to confirm my inspiration from the records, yet my designs harmonized perfectly with the costumes of the Mosaic period—because, I believe, I had remembered them.'[37] The fertility of his imagination seemed to surprise him. Ferragamo felt like an instrument in others' hands. A medium between worlds, beings, an entity floating on an eternal tide. His 'wedge shoes' were created in 1936 when, because of the war in Ethiopia, the steel used to reinforce the sole in the area of the plantar arch was not available: 'Without the proper steel I could not make shoes to my special fitting, yet my reputation was founded on my fitting. [...] I sat and experimented with pieces of Sardinian cork, pushing and glueing and fixing and trimming until the entire space between the sole and the heel was blocked solid. At last one pair was finished—the modern world's first pair of "wedgies".'[38] The history of the so-called *lifties*—this was the name given by Manuel Gerton to those shoes—is tinged with a very interesting note: 'At the time of its invention the "wedgie" was hailed as "completely new," as "utterly different," as "a revolution." But in 1949 workmen escavating the ruins of Boccaccio's villa, near Florence, unearthed some shoes worn by his women friends. They were wedgies—clumsy, heavy, and ugly wedgies, but wedgies nevertheless. My "revolution" was at least six hundred years old. Perhaps in a previous existence upon this earth I designed them and in my new life remembered them.'[39]

KRISHNAMURTI IN CALIFORNIA

The 'Shoemaker to the Stars' spoke of memories and inspirations that never corresponded to experiences or artistic encounters of his youth or childhood. He met people from all over the world, great figures of the 20th century, but he did not cite painters, sculptors, poets or writers. In the necessary moments, however, he lived through experiences far removed in time and in space, channels of communication with archetypes opened up to him; he travelled back in history. Inspired by these clear visions, from the return of memory, Ferragamo proceeded to invent new combinations of forms and colours: he worked with a speed that is typical of those who act in a creative trance. One had the impression of running into the tip of an iceberg. Below the surface of the story philosophical and human knowledge was palpitating that was much more complex than what emerged in the autobiography. It is very likely, then, that he had spiritual experiences of a certain significance between 1917 and 1927, during his long stay in America, in Santa Barbara and in Hollywood. Perhaps some metaphysical questions matured in him after the death of his brother Elio, who died following a car accident in which Salvatore himself was driving, or during his long period in hospital, when Ferragamo had been recovering from the injuries suffered in that tragic accident. Or else, we may assume that Salvatore Ferragamo had heard talk of reminiscence, immortality, golden section, cosmic flow, *karma* and illusions on returning to Italy, to Florence from 1927, which, as it is known, was the cradle of hermetics, Neo-Pythagoreans and Neoplatonists since the time of the 'Academy of Careggi.' Due to strange coincidences, prestigious actors and directors, whom Ferragamo knew, met and spent unforgettable time with Jiddu Krishnamurti, the young 'Alcione,' the 'son of Krishna,' whom Annie Besant, chairperson of the International Theosophical Society, had adopted in India in 1909, introducing him to her associates as the third Saviour of the world. In the Twenties the 'Buddha Maitreya' was in California in the Ojai Valley, not far from Santa Barbara and from Hollywood, where he had a mystical crisis in contact with the wild and uncontaminated nature of the location. The aura of the Indian master probably came to be felt in the more cultured and elegant environments of cinema and the US aristocracy, those frequented by the very young Ferragamo. In a photograph from those years, alongside Krishnamurti we seem to be able to recognise the already mentioned Cecil B. DeMille, together with an actor wearing an ancient costume. As we have already said, Ferragamo worked for DeMille during a number of major productions (*The Ten Commandments, The King of Kings*). John Barrymore was also a customer of Salvatore; he was a handsome and tormented actor, a convinced Buddhist, in contact with the American Theosophical Society through his agent's wife. It seems that on at least in two occasions Barrymore, nicknamed 'the Great Profile,' met the young 'star of the East,' even proposing that he participate in a film on the life of Buddha. Another Californian episode confirms to us the respect and admiration that extraordinary personalities from the world of movies and literature felt for the fascinating Indian master. It is said that Aldous Huxley, Charlie Chaplin and Greta Garbo met with Krishnamurti for a *déjeuner sur l'herbe* in Ojai. It would be interesting to know the subjects discussed during that rustic conversation. Something important

must have been recorded by those people's hearts. It is sufficient to listen with greater attention to the famous final speech by Chaplin in *The Great Dictator* to see that behind the appeal to 'universal brotherhood' there is perhaps the memory of Ojai.

Aldous Huxley, the author of masterpieces of science fiction such as *Brave New World* and *The Island*, the real spiritual father of the 'flower children,' lived in Italy between 1923 and 1930, and set two of his stories in Florence and Rome. Huxley was to meet Krishnamurti a number of times and go deeply into spiritual matters, transcendence and Hindu mysticism set against the alienation of modern man: alienation provoked, in his view, by the development of technology and by the use that was to be made of it by the international organisations of power, both political and economic. Greta Garbo was one of the most affectionate customers of Ferragamo, who met the diva many times, admiring her exceptional talent and charisma, the power and fascination of her personality.[40]

Examining Krishnamurti's biography in detail, we discover that he was in Florence on a number of occasions (the evidence of this is a portrait executed by painter Giovanni Costetti, as Luca Scarlini points out in this publication): a first time in 1937, when he had already severed his ties with the Theosophical Society, putting an end to the experience of the Order of the Star (1911–29); then in 1953,[41] again hosted on the hills of Fiesole by Vanda Scaravelli, the Florentine noblewoman and pianist, well known for having practised and taught yoga, and by Alberto Passigli, her father, an eminent personality in the city's cultural life, who, among other things, in 1919 founded the society of the Amici della Musica, and then, the Orchestra Stabile Fiorentina, the true point of departure of the future Maggio Musicale Fiorentino. We must also remember that Passigli participated in the publishing adventure of *Il Mondo* magazine—the periodical thought up in 1945 by Alessandro Bonsanti, with personalities of the calibre of Arturo Loria, Eugenio Montale and Luigi Scaravelli, the philosopher and Vanda's husband.[42]

The influence of Krishnamurti was even felt in Hollywood in the most cultured and elegant environments of cinema. In this photograph from the Twenties, alongside Krishnamurti, is director Cecil B. DeMille with an actor wearing an ancient costume

Greta Garbo and John Barrymore photographed on January 28th 1932 backstage at the film *Grand Hotel*. Both had shown interest for Oriental culture and had been charmed by the personality of guru Jiddu Krishnamurti

SYNCRETISMS

As we know, hermetism and esoterism, Kabbalah and Alchemy, intersections between Western and Oriental philosophies, Sufism and magic have always been at home in Florence. And to some extent these syncretisms have always been opposed. Some masterpieces of the Renaissance and of Hermetism conserved in the city were re-studied at the end of the 19th century (for instance by Aby Warburg) as emblems of the rebirth of paganism, and the memory that has never waned of the theses of Marsilio Ficino, of Poliziano and of Pico della Mirandola once again nourished polemics, rekindled by feelings of aversion towards scientism and materialism.

In 1906–07—more or less in the period in which he perfected his vision of 'Man-God' together with that of magical pragmatism—Giovanni Papini made the pages of *Leonardo* available for the publication of essays devoted to mysticism, to irrationalist Romanticism, to theosophy and even to occultism and magic (he was criticised for this by US philosopher William James). That periodical, founded by Papini ('Gian Falco') with Giuseppe Prezzolini ('Giuliano il Sofista') in 1903, came about in the wake of a renewed cult of authors such as Novalis, Nietzsche and Schopenhauer, together with that for authors closer in time such as Rudolf Steiner, Spencer, James and Bergson (we read there, for instance, that the creators 'in ART love the ideal transfiguration of life and combat its inferior forms, they aspire to beauty as evocative figuration and revelation of a profound and serene life'). Other protagonists of the Florentine cultural life of those years were the frequenters of the Biblioteca Filosofica (or Teosofica) in Piazza Donatello, including Arturo Reghini, a fascinating personality (he was almost two metres tall) and a man of vast culture, who was to write on more than one occasion precisely in *Leonardo*. The Biblioteca, founded in 1905 by a tight group of scholars, and with the contribution of the American Julia H. Scott, had, according to Eugenio Garin, 'theosophical and magical origins, which were well in tune with a certain cultural climate of the first decade of the century. [...] And from a certain perspective it could be said that the Biblioteca Filosofica with its core of books and magazines, with its discussions, with its cycles of lessons and lectures, tended to take shape as an institute, as a sort of free faculty of philosophical and religious studies, those cultural, idealistic, spiritualistic, modernist positions that in some way polemised against the official university tradition.'[43] Arturo Reghini (1878–1946) was one of the greatest scholars of Pythagoras (the prestigious *Dei Numeri Pitagorici*, in seven volumes, is by him), whom he had been introduced to by Amedeo Armetano. From Reghini's mind there germinated, among other things, a work on *Dante e il linguaggio segreto dei Fedeli d'Amore* and an article on *Androgino Ermetico*. He also translated *De Occulta Philosophia* by Cornelius Agrippa and *Le Roi du Monde* by René Guénon. He published in various periodicals of the time, among which, in addition to the already cited *Leonardo*, mention should be made of *Ur* magazine, founded by Julius Evola (1898–1974), in which texts by Giamblico, Pico della Mirandola, Gustav Meyrink (a pseudonym of Gustav Meyer) and even by Milarepa also appeared. For a short period, Reghini also worked with the editorial board of *Lacerba*.[44] A short distance from Palazzo Spini Feroni the fundamental episode in Reghini's life occurred, a kind of mystical ecstasy that led him to understand the true nature of the self and the connection between individual soul and universal soul, between earthly existence and cosmic flow.[45]

But let us return to Giovanni Papini to reconstruct briefly a historical framework that is reliable, but also significant for non academic studies. On the pages of *Leonardo*,[46] the young writer, philosopher and already a polemicist, called for the return of the Medieval: 'The magicians, the occultists, the spirits, the ghosts, the spectres return from the distant shadows; the mystics return; the saints reappear and even Catholicism arises again. This begins to concern the doctors of medicine and surgery and the humanitarian lawyers and also the schoolteachers, who arch their brows, and the rationalists shake their heads.' Consider that in 1903 Gian Falco–Papini had organised a 'spectral' conference at the Florentine Ethnological Museum on the subject of magic and demonology, and in 1911 he had oriented the short life of the magazine *Anima*, founded together with Giovanni Amendola, in the direction of theosophy.

We must also remember that Giovanni Papini participated in the international congress of philosophy that took place in Bologna, again in 1911, where Rudolf Steiner had been invited to present the principles of his anthroposophic doctrine. It would be worthwhile to dig into the Florentine culture of the first decades of the 20th century, to understand up to what point and in which of the appointed places questions of a metaphysical-esoteric type had been faced. Not least, the early inclusion in local culture of questions of sacred science, those publicised by René Guénon, and of anthroposophy, considering that the theses of Rudolf Steiner, as we just see, were already widespread in Florence in the early years of the 20th century. We repeat, however, that religious and philosophical syncretism, theosophy, were subjects used in those decades against materialism and rationalism, to tackle the incipient domination of mechanistic civilisation, and to combat the alienation of the best human faculties in capitalist society.[47] This reasoning also included the defence of the *artifex*, that of handicraft traditions still tied to the world of the most ancient symbols and ancient

of his originality as a poet and a playwright, within the esoteric current of Symbolism. In *Le Roi Bombance*, a play conceived in 1905—embellished by the sets by theosophic painter Paul E. Ronson—Marinetti creates a complex political allegory based on reincarnation, a theme barely considered by the French Symbolist poets.'[49] At a certain point in the show, Marinetti even had a monologue recited by a lunar phantasm, 'a direct paraphrase of the famous passage of the *Bhagavad-Gita* on the principles of primordial unity: "I am Death in Life, joined [...] before the eternal reality of nature, I am the absolute and unique force that always remains identical to itself".' In this case, the young Marinetti used Hindu and Buddhist texts to 'designate the fatal revival of the past in the eternal and deceptive regeneration of life.'[50] Traces of these inspirations are obviously found in various early 20th century artistic and literary environments,[51] undoubtedly in Futurism (in one of the first manifestos we read: 'Who can still believe in the opacity of bodies, while our acute and multiple sensibility makes us sense the dark manifestations of medianic phenomena? Why must we continue to create without taking account of our visual power, which can give similar results to those of X-rays?') and then, but with great differences, in early Surrealism.

alchemies. Perhaps also for this reason, our Ferragamo chose Florence as his ideal destination, stimulated by a creative and productive environment that was still based on the wisdom of the hands, as an antithesis to the civilisation of machines.

ALTERATIONS AND OTHERNESS

In 1904 Filippo Tommaso Marinetti—the pyrotechnical founder of Futurism, the great haranguer and cultural agitator—published a long poem, *La Momie sanglante*, inspired by the *Egyptian Book of the Dead*. In that period the young Marinetti launched the magazine *Poesia* in Milan; he also had a 'friendship in Paris with occultist poet Jules Bois, and participated assiduously in spiritualist sessions that the medium Melina organised in the home of writer Enrico Annibale Butti, again in Milan.'[48] It is interesting, then, to follow the analysis that Giovanni Lista, the scholar of Futurism and the European avant-garde, makes of this period: 'At the time, Marinetti was in direct contact with the Parisian environments of late Symbolism, characterised in particular by esoterism and by "occult sciences," but his work draws above all from his childhood in Egypt. His lawyer father, who was a passionate scholar of the history of religions, had initiated him early in this type of reading, so as to enable him at times to distance himself, or to give evidence

MOVIE FRAMES OF FUTURIST LIFE

Let's tackle the kaleidoscopic futurist world. In 1916, in Piazza della Signoria and Piazzale Michelangelo, a movie was filmed entitled *Vita futurista*. The author of that experimental work was Count Arnaldo Ginanni Corradini. Acting in that first avant-garde film were: Marinetti, Giacomo Balla, the director himself and his brother Bruno. The actors play at provoking the spectators, with phantasmatic and anamorphic apparitions aroused 'by the medianic waves of a dance.'[52] In many ways those dissolutions of the dancing figures into the ether are reminiscent of the vorticisms and the bright spirals of Loïe Fuller, the 'fairy of light,' as she appears for instance in a short film by the Lumière brothers. The history of Arnaldo Ginna (this was the pseudonym that Count Ginanni Corradini was to assume when adhering to Futurism) from Ravenna is particularly interesting. Ginna arrived in Florence in 1909, and joined an avant-garde group founded by Virginio Scattolini, Mario Carli, Remo Chiti and Emilio Settimelli. Through the magazines *Difesa dell'arte*, *Il centauro* and *Rivista d'arte e di vita*, the group promoted 'cerebrist art,' a type of language that emerged from the study of cerebral energy as such, unhooked from the obstacles of the logical spirit.[53] These 'cerebrists' tested themselves in an expression 'rich in theosophy and metapsychic allusions'.[54] Ginna was passionate about 'the work of Alfred Kubin and the drawings of

Portrait of Filippo Tommaso Marinetti, the Futurist poet. The photo is from 1911. In the background, allusive references to the Oriental world. In Paris Marinetti was in direct contact with the environments of late Symbolism, characterised by esoterism. But his work drew from his childhood in Egypt, where his father had introduced him to the history of religions

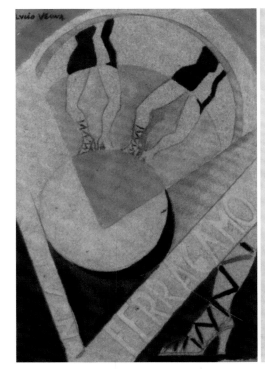 

In the sketches and the advertising poster created for Ferragamo in 1930, Lucio Venna mixed photographic objectivity and German design with Graeco-Roman evocations. The model *Coturno* is a sandal with variable lacing for beach, for walking and for the home: a multi-purpose shoe, an affirmation of the Italian style that we would like to compare with the overalls by Ernesto Michahelles, known as Thayaht.
Coturno Ferragamo, **advertising sketch, 1930 Pencil and watercolour on cardboard, 20.3 x 30.5 cm Florence, Salvatore Ferragamo Museum**
Coturno Ferragamo, **1930 Chromolithography on paper, 100 x 135 cm Treviso, Museo Civico L. Bailo, Salce Collection**

the alienated. His brother, Bruno Corra, with a literary temperament, was a theorist interested in the experimental sciences. The two Dioscuri frequented an academy of artists in Ravenna catalysed by the medium Franco Passi, who 'practises medianic writing, organises spiritualist sessions and experiences of telekinesis.'[55]

The chronicles tell us that Lucio Venna (Giuseppe Landsmann) participated in the realisation of Ginna's film as assistant director; Venna was a Venetian painter who arrived in the Tuscan capital in 1912, just in time to be present at the first Futurist exhibition of *Lacerba* organised in 1913 at the Gonnelli bookshop and to immediately join the movement, following other Florentine artists (including Primo Conti, Ottone Rosai, Emilio Notte). Subsequently Venna worked with Bruno Corra and Emilio Settimelli providing designs and 'parolibere' for their magazine *L'Italia Futurista* and participated in group exhibitions (for instance, the *Great National Futurist Exhibition* of 1919 planned by Marinetti in Milan, where Venna exhibited together with Balla, Russolo, Depero, Sironi, Cangiullo and others). In around 1930 he abandoned painting to devote himself exclusively to advertising graphics. He created extraordinary posters, among the most elegant and fantasy-filled in Europe. In that period Venna came into contact with Salvatore Ferragamo, for whom he created a poster and a pamphlet to publicise new models. On the project sheets there are Classical names: *Pompeiana, Nemi, Sparta* and a more contemporary title, *Moderne*. Another banner was invented by Venna, mixing photographic objectivity and German design with Graeco-Roman suggestions. This advertising was designed to

launch a model with 'variable lacing for the beach, for walking and for the home.' It is the *Coturno Ferragamo*, an archetypal, multi-purpose shoe, an affirmation of Italian style that we would like to compare, for its simplicity (of spirit and function) with the very famous *Tuta* or overalls by Ernesto Michahelles—known as Thayaht. In the manifesto for Ferragamo 'a shapely, bold female figure, ball and costume, designs the diagonal of the sheet, invading, with the pointed yellow leg, the black central circle that contains the footwear. Below, on the black rectangle, the illumination of the owner of the company is ignited.'[56] The culture of Ferragamo is communicated perfectly with a grammar that brings out distant origins and new originality. These are balanced yet lively images, where vanishing lines and perspectives of a Futurist type are combined with a more orderly geometric planning, circular and winding elements, straight lines and acute angles; a chromatic concert of colours, now solar and Mediterranean, now artificial and urban, to communicate energy and happiness, health and harmony. We perceive, in short, a return of Aeolian rhythms, of large and serene proportions, classical emotions and sensations, yet immersed in a communicative language that now cannot help but take account of the conquests of modern life, with its tensions and accelerations, more Dionysian than Apollinean.

APOLLON MUSAGÈTE IN OVERALLS

In some period photos, Thayaht appears as young and beautiful as a Greek god, midway between Apollon Musagète and Dionysus, with features of an American actor and the spirit of a Parisian dandy. Influenced by Paul Gauguin, he was always to go in search of a being and an appearance that was simple, archaic, fully in tune with universal nature. Painter, sculptor, designer and inventor of the very famous *Tuta*, Thayaht also worked with Madame Vionnet in Paris from 1918, where he also designed the logo of the Transalpine stylist, drawing inspiration from the poses and costumes of Isadora Duncan and Vaslav Nijinsky. Here he crossed paths with the Ballets Russes and came into contact with the musical and artistic environment of the avant-gardes. After the Forties, Thayaht retired to Marina di Pietrasanta to devote himself, in the latter period of his life, to the study of astronomy, seeking evidence of life in the cosmos. And in Versilia, Ernesto Michahelles passed away in 1959, placating his tormented spirit with visions and spiritual communications that were not transitory or worldly. On the other hand, since the Twenties Thayaht had reduced his interest in a certain Futurist language, which was too tied to the exaltation of modernity and its technological or political myths, to move closer rather to

.THAYAHT.
9, Via Dante da Castiglione
FIRENZE, 34 - Italia

.THAYAHT.
9, Via Dante da Castiglione
FIRENZE, 34 - Italia

Fuchsia
et violet.

Henriette

.THAYAHT.
9, Via Dante da Castiglione
FIRENZE, 34 - Italia

.THAYAHT.
9, Via Dante da Castiglione
FIRENZE, 34 - Italia

Painter, sculptor, designer and inventor of the very famous *Tuta* or overalls, Thayaht worked with Madame Vionnet in Paris from 1918. Thayaht, *Sketches for dresses*, fashion sketches for dresses by Madeleine Vionnet, 1921–24 Pencil and watercolour on paper, 20 x 26 cm Lucca, Private Collection

the study of Abstractism and to deepen the 'spiritual in art.' In this regard, his Parisian contacts were decisive, and perhaps also his direct knowledge of the works of Sonia Delaunay, his reading of the theoretical texts of Kandinsky and early consideration of the work carried out in the Weimar school, particularly the research into forms and colours by Johannes Itten. Starting from the discovery and reinterpretation of a manuscript text by Thayaht from 1919, Mauro Pratesi[57] reconstructs a line of very particular interests. The scholar makes reference to the artistic theories of Denman Ross and the studies by Jay Hambidge 'on dynamic symmetry, which the famous scholar had divulged, incidentally, on the pages of the magazine founded by him, *The Diagonal*, which Thayaht possessed and had read and carefully annotated.'[58] To these names he adds that of Claude Bragdon and writes: 'The thread running through that connected all these studies and disparate experiences was interest in the mystical content of art, the symbology of colours, harmony in painting, the concept of the abstract in art, the esoteric and Orientalist philosophies associated with Theosophy. This doctrine, which had grown up around the theories of Péladan's *Rose-Croix* movement, acquired widespread popularity in the early 20th century thanks to the dissemination of these by Rudolf Steiner, whose books, as is known, Kandinsky had read and whose lectures he had listened to, remaining very much influenced where the theosophist indicated the work of the artist as a raising of everyday life onto the spiritual plane, releasing the content from physical reality'.[59] At a certain point Pratesi evokes 'theosophical, occult and esoteric doctrines'[60] that were to prompt Thayaht to 'create, before the war, the first non-figurative "colour compositions," understood as abstract harmonies,'[61] such as in *Paesaggio spaziale* and *Thoughts of Construction* from 1914. And then a letter dated 1918 'sent to the well known theorist of psychism from London W. J. Crawford, to whom [Thayaht] reports that he has read his book *Reality of Psychic Phenomena* with passion and that he appreciates his experiments with the Goligher Circle.'[62] In that letter 'Thayaht defined himself as rather subject to telepathy, with a sensitive and nervous temperament; he reported on his telepathic experiments and declared, furthermore, that he was a passionate reader of Tagore, Mantegazza, Bergson, Maeterlinck and others.'[63] This esoteric cultural mould would be explained, again according to Pratesi, by the time spent by the young Thayaht with the Braggiottis: 'fervent believers' in spiritualist doctrines, in reincarnation, convinced vegetarians, who 'demonised the killing of insects and the cutting of flowers' and 'loved surrounding themselves every day with artists and intellectuals with whom to read pages from the *Bhagavad-Gita*.'[64] The same text, incidentally, that had conditioned Marinetti.

Thayaht's interest in esoteric doctrines led him to also subsequently take an interest in astronomy, as shown by this painting from 1932, *Paesaggio spaziale (Spatial landscape)* (pastel, coloured pencil on cardboard, 22 x 25 cm. Florence, Sandro Michahelles Collection), testimony to his eclecticism

3 | INSPIRATION

'The sun has the width of a human foot.' Heraclitus

ILLUMINATION[65]

Modernity in the 20th century, as we know, begins in this way: when the artist discovers new materials, new techniques and new systems of presentation. Fashion is involved in this semantic opening, in the discovery of greater expressive possibilities. 'There is no limit to beauty,' Ferragamo said with the same certainty of avant-garde artists, 'no saturation point in design, no end to the materials a shoemaker may use to decorate his creations so that every woman may be shod like a princess and a princess may be shod like a fairy queen. There is no limit to the materials I have used in these fifty years of shoemaking. [...] I have used diamonds and pearls, real and imitation; gold and silver dust; fine leather from Germany, Britain, America, and wherever else they may be found. I have used satins and silks, lace and needlework, glass and glass mirrors, feathers, the skins of ostrich, antelope, kangaroo, leopard, lizard, python, water snakes, and even more weird and strange reptiles. I have used fish, felt, and transparent paper, snail shells and raffia, synthetic silk woven instead of raffia, raw silk, seaweeds and wool. I have used *petit point* and *petit point* raffia, taffeta and Manila hemp, nickel alloy and iridescent kid, velvet and linen, webbing and suede. I have used beads, sequins, nylon [...] and transparent paper "straw," which is string covered by transparent paper.'[66] In Hollywood he also happened to

have to satisfy the demands of an Indian princess and invented shoes decorated with the feathers of small hummingbirds.

The account provided by Ferragamo resembles that compiled by a young student of Bauhaus few years before. We are in around 1927 and Alfredo Bortoluzzi (Karlsruhe 1905 – Peschici 1995) follows the preparatory course by Josef Albers (1888–1976) in Dessau, remaining surprised by the experimentation with materials. Albers' courses were far from traditional courses, but carried forward with academic rigour: 'On the first day'—remembers Bortoluzzi many years later—'they gave me a sheet of paper without any implement. The lesson was: the paper can be folded up and torn with the hands: later the paper can be cut with scissors: the paper can be smooth or rough; the sensitivity for the material grows by touching the various materials; velvet, in contrast with sandpaper, leather, metal, rope, wire wool. This is how *Materialenstudien* came about: the collages, first chaotic, later more refined; with cellophane, voile, tracing paper, lace, woollen yarn, etc.'[67] Added to the variety of raw materials were experimentations into colours and compositional types ('optical gradations of the material, for example with close or loose mesh, transparent-opaque, clear-dark-dense'[68]) taken from nature from geometry or the unconscious.

Years earlier, the Futurists had expressed the same painterly freedom. In 1909, in the Parisian daily newspaper *Le Figaro*, Marinetti shouted: 'We want to sing the love of danger, the habit of energy and temerity, courage, audacity, rebellion, will be essential elements of our poetry.' Futurism, explains the already quoted Giovanni Lista, is not only painting or literature; it is 'a revolutionary movement that sets itself the task of establishing in general a new sensibility and a new approach to the world and to art in particular.'[69] In other words, says the historian, it is an anthropological project, with which Marinetti and company seek to 'rethink man in his comparison with the world of machines, speed and technology.'[70] The futurists, that is, propose the myth of the total work of art; they desire 'to reinvent daily life, through art,'[71] intercepting every sphere of human activities: fashion, design, toys, graphic and typographic creation, furnishings, behaviour, sport, politics, cinema, advertising, etc.

In 1914, on the pages of *Lacerba*, Giovanni Papini, surprised by the first insertions of heterogeneous objects, had written: 'For now we are only at the beginning. [...] But if the method takes hold and is pushed to its ultimate, most rigorous consequences, it would follow that the best still-life painting is a furnished room; the best concert all the noises of a populous city.'[72] The more fiery Boccioni, one of the founders of

Like the Futurists and the avant-garde artists, Ferragamo was fascinated by experimentation with materials, from the richest and most exotic, used with new techniques of workmanship, to the poorest, which he was to use especially in autarkic period in Italy, such as in this model shoe made in patchwork felt in 1935–38 Florence, Salvatore Ferragamo Museum

Giacomo Balla, *Auto in corsa (Running car)*, 1930 Oil and enamel on wood panel, 44 x 30 cm Florence, Private Collection. With their art the Futurists proposed an anthropological project; they rethought man in his contact with the world of cars, speed and technology

Futurism in painting, had responded to the Florentine writer explaining that the modern artist, 'to escape the imitative procedure that makes him inevitably fall into the most well-worn appearances, replaces its very reality.'[73] A short time would pass and Giacomo Balla was to account for the *Complessi plastici* specifying the 'poli-material' and 'poli-expressive' components deployed by the avant-garde: 'Threads of wire, cotton, silk wool, of every thickness, highly coloured, mirror fabrics, metallic sheets, coloured tinfoil and all garish substances.'[74] Balla already spoke in terms of total art, of the convergence between the real world and the space of art. The sculptural object—with the craftsman prey to perceptive dynamism and seeking one-to-one presentations of daily objects—was to escape the base imposed on the monument according to the more academic canons. Marinetti had no doubts: 'Before us art was memory, the sorrowful re-evocation of a lost Object (happiness, love, landscape). [...] With Futurism, on the contrary, art becomes art-action. [...] Art becomes Presence, new Object, new Reality created with the abstract elements of the universe.'[75] The closeness between art and fashion also passed through the use of unprecedented materials, in the common sharing of the everyday, of natural and modern elements removed from reality and history with imaginative takes and powerful spiritual needs.

Thus, in a painting from 1914 Enrico Prampolini enjoys a tailor's repertoire (crinoline, feathers, silk). With *Béquinage* the artist alludes to femininity and the woman's body with elegance and seduction, putting the gaze in contact with personal effects above the skin and below the clothing, to fill the contemplation with erotic tension. The work in question seems created following the instructions of the *Manifesto tecnico della scultura* by Umberto Boccioni, written in 1912. Here we read: 'In a Futurist sculptural composition [we will have] wood or metal surfaces, immobile or mechanically mobile, for an object, hairy spherical forms for the hair, semicircles of glass for a vase, iron wire and grilles for an atmospheric plane.'[76] In tune with Boccioni, the older Balla used mirrors, tinfoil, talc, cardboard and wire to create a strange sculpture that he entitled *Complesso plastico colorato di linee forza*. At the same time Umberto Boccioni gave form to the *Dinamismo di un cavallo in corsa+case* using cardboard and painted iron, as, in other works (today sadly lost) he used fragments in porcelain and women's hair. The Futurists knew how to move. Planes and figures in a painting were arranged freely like words and vice versa. With the same freedom different materials can be taken and used. 'For me a Futurist painting'—wrote Carlo Carrà in his autobiography—'did not reside in *Lefranc* tubes. If

an individual possesses an expressive sense, whatever he creates, driven by this sense, will always be in the domain of painting. Wood, paper, fabric, leather, glass, rope, waxed cloth, majolica, metals, colours, putty, words (consonants, vowels and numbers) enter our artistic conceptions as strongly legitimate materials.'[77]

A HOUSE OF FUTURIST ART

Giacomo Balla and Fortunato Depero, who in 1915 drafted their manifesto entitled *Ricostruzione futurista dell'universo*, had clear ideas on the freedom of media and on the variety of materials. The two proposed a full-blown irregular repertoire: 'Threads of metal, cotton, wool, silk of every thickness. Coloured glass, carbon paper, celluloid, metal grilles, coloured tinfoil and all garish substances. Mechanical, electro-technical, musical and noise-making devices; chemically luminous liquids of variable colourations: springs; levers; pipes.'[78] Science, technology, game and irony were interpenetrated to unhinge the rules of sculpture. Balla and Depero imagined to create kinetic works (the reference was to Balla's 'mobile plastic complex') and 'artificial living beings.' The cases of Balla and Depero were undoubtedly among the most emblematic, we need only think that the former was to be the creator of items of clothing that became famous, of furniture and room decorations, while the other was to move with uninhibited ingeniousness and entrepreneurial capacity between art, theatre, advertising and design, inventing advertising campaigns, covers for magazines (in America his whimsical images were to appear in *Vogue*, *Vanity Fair*, *The New Yorker* and *Sparks*), the famous bottle of the aperitif Campari in 1923 (a painting-poster *Squisito Selz* was displayed at the 1926 Venice Biennale) and the advertising for the liqueur Strega. Among Depero's many experiences we may recall the theatre, the fabric paintings and the tapestries. As regards his association with theatre, this took shape in a text entitled *Colori* and in the meeting with Sergei Diaghilev (1872–1929), the great entrepreneur of the Ballets Russes, for which Depero executed a set design project and many preparatory designs of costumes.[79] *Colori* is a theatrical synthesis conceived 'in the area of *Gestaltpsychologie*: the actors were in fact missing, replaced by "abstract individualities," immersed in a scenic-colour space. These abstract entities had a phono-chromatic character, in the sense that they emitted sounds that took shape as colour forms.'[80]

Weaving, alongside collage, became a field of action for many Futurist, Cubo-Futurist and Orphic artists. Depero is not less important than his French or German colleagues. With pieces of coloured cloth Depero created collage since 1917, then with time, under the attentive and expert guidance of Rosetta, the artist's wife, a certain number of assistants created works of large dimensions for him, activating an idea and a practice in art that was as futuristic as ever. The greatest invention by Fortunato Depero was nevertheless his *Casa d'Arte Futurista*, where tapestries, advertising posters, furniture and other furnishing objects were produced. 'In fact, the spirit of *Ricostruzione futurista dell'universo*, with its kaleidoscopic array of proposals, certainly could not remain caged in the sphere of galleries and museums, or be practised in sterile experimentations, both striking and ephemeral. And, given his strong operational personality, the ideal test bench for verifying the actual proliferation of the Futurist idea could not but be that of the applied arts.'[81]

FUTUR-BALLA. A PAINTING WALKS IN THE CROWD

'The painter Balla, born in Turin in 1871, without concerning himself with schools and masters, immediately devoted himself to the search for truth, interpreting its infinite aspects with a colour-spherical and luminous technique / the painting. FAILURE / and many portraits reached an expressive, almost palpating reality, an impressive clarity and relief. At 40 he abandoned celebrity honours interests to devote himself to his Futurist research. First with the analytical study of things in movement in the painting: *Cane al guinzaglio*, then speed and interpenetration in the painting: *Automobili in corsa* and then into the forms of thought in the painting: *Pessimismo ottimismo*. After 16 years of inexhaustible resistance, this new sensibility (expression of art) has created a style that begins to be revealed everywhere in Decorative art, in fashion, in furniture, in architecture, in posters, etc. etc.'[82]

Balla's career began with the study of the possible relations between art and science, in search of an objectivity beyond Impressionism. The artist was interested in photography, also thanks to the example of his father, and therefore in research into the movement of bodies and objects conducted by the photographers of the time (in particular Eadweard Muybridge and Etienne J. Marey).[83] Before his meeting with Marinetti, the painterly language to which Balla made reference was that of Italian Divisionism and of French *Pointillisme*, studied in Paris in 1900–01. In Turin, where he attended the Accademia Sabauda, he came into contact with Pellizza da Volpedo in 1891. He was also to look with admiration at the work of Segantini and Previati, from whom, however, he was separated by the search for an objectivity not filled with symbolism and religious

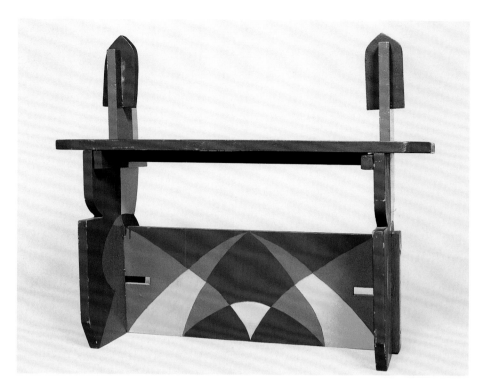

transcendence. Balla interpreted the destructive energy of Futurism, converting it in a playful way: he wanted to express a playful and creative idea of existence, which, though moving from a deep knowledge of the new scientific theories (those, for example, on colour and light) and from an admiration for the discoveries of technology (lighting, cinema, the automobile), was open to daily poetry, admitting among his spheres that of the banal and the ephemeral. After paintings such as *Lampada ad arco* from 1909 or 1911, in which the romantic motif of moonlight is overpowered by the light of a modern electric lamp, Balla constructed abstract paintings such as the famous *Compenetrazioni iridescenti* (already experimented with in 1912, as proven by a postcard that the artist sent from Düsseldorf to Gino Galli, a student of his). In these works, Balla articulates an abstract landscape, with repeated colours on a structure of triangular forms, which he called a 'type of iris.' These were works marked by a conceptual, already optical procedure, where the analysis of the enigma of colour and light does not stiffen into schematic or too explanatory transpositions, but tends to venture into geometry and modulations with fantasy and lyricism, in a playful, fantastic function. According to some interpreters of Balla, this series of works came about from the knowledge of the so-called pyramid of philosopher and mathematician Johann Heinrich Lambert (1728–1777), whose theories Balla could have discovered during his stay in Germany, together, obviously, with Etienne J. Marey's chrono-photographs. This research of his was differentiated from that conducted by certain abstract

Giacomo Balla, *Futur Panca (Futurist bench)*, 1925
Painted wood,
69 x 78.3 x 25.3 cm
Prato, Farsettiarte Collection

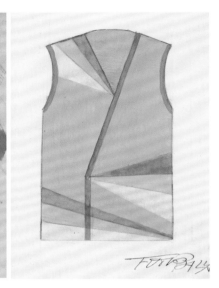

painters, who in his view were still interested in the ideation of museum art, of paintings to hang framed. In contrast, the Italian artist aimed at a clearcut broadening of horizons, both linguistic and behavioural, with a view to a collaboration between art and life, between fine arts and applied arts. We find among the first incarnations of Balla's new credo the print on a tie with geometric-abstract motifs, structured and coloured in the manner of *Compenetrazioni iridescenti*: 'A painting to carry, mobile and ephemeral, that is, on the scale of daily life.'[84] On the subject of these inventions, Louis Corpechot wrote in the newspapers of the time: 'Balla wears a Futurist tie, a green and yellow knot that has the form of the propeller of an aeroplane, Futurist white and yellow shoes.'[85] It seems to see a painting walking in the crowd, what the Futurists imagined they would obtain with all the means at their disposal.

Expanding in every direction, Balla's Futurist interventionism moved towards the designing of environments, furnishings, scenographies, furniture, for a total renewal of space and common objects. Of particular interest is the study of clothing, for a 'genre of surprise decoration, focusing on the vivacity of forms and colours to create the irruption of evocative life-affirming and playful elements in the rhythms of daily existence.'[86]

BLACK BOOKS IN COLOUR

Paris, Twenties. On a visiting card promoting a studio in Boulevard Malesherbes we read: 'Sonia Delaunay. Robes, manteau, écharpes, sacs, tapis, tissus simultanés.' A key exponent of Orphic Cubism and Abstraction, Sonia Terk Delaunay (1885–1979) was one of the most interesting figures of the Parisian avant-garde. Her battleground, as it was for Balla, was

undoubtedly applied arts, with the aim of connecting the world of colour with that of life, through an eclectic production of objects and scenic situations. Starting with research into primary colours, geometries, ornamental composition, simultaneity, she dedicated herself to the creation of fabrics for clothing and textiles for the home, draperies and carpets, costumes for the theatre, without ever abandoning painterly and graphic ideation. Arriving in Paris in 1906, soon afterwards Sonia married Robert Delaunay and together with her husband gave rise to Orphic Cubism. She worked with Diaghilev and the Ballets Russes and very soon (1910–11) she created 'unique pieces in which she combined different materials (the patchwork bedspread for the cradle of her son Charles, waistcoats, overcoats and her "simultaneous dress").'[87] Already in 1913 Delaunay began her abstract research into colour and light, into simultaneity and free expression. In 1925 she worked

with Robert in the planning of decorative panels for the Universal Exposition in Paris and designed the layout of the *Boutique Simultanée* in association with Jacques Heim, imagining the opening of branches in London and Rio de Janeiro. On the topic of the simultaneous term and the concept of simultaneity, a polemic was triggered with Futurist painters, who, when they arrived in Paris for their first exhibition in 1912 at the Galerie Bernheim-Jeune, had to answer to Robert and Sonia Delaunay,[88] who were far from willing to acknowledge any claim the Italian troupe had to that discovery. It was a real war of ideological positions and poetics, sparked to better define a new extension of the contemporary, with its unprecedented horizons and its unexplored dimensions.[89] The greatest theorist of the avant-garde of that time, Guillaume Apollinaire, coining the term 'Orphic Cubism' and isolating the characteristic aspects of that style, wrote that it was about 'new compositions with elements drawn not from visual reality, but entirely created by the artist and endowed with a mighty reality. The works of Orphic artists must simultaneously offer a pure aesthetic pleasure, a construction that hits the senses and a sublime meaning, that is the subject. It is pure art.'[90] Sonia dates a work, *Simultaneous Contrasts*, in 1912, while Robert, again in 1912, opens his *Windows* and gives rise to his *Simultaneous Contrasts: Sun and Moon*. In 1913 the painter Sonia created *La prose du Transsibérien et de la petite Jehanne de France (Prose of Trans-Siberian and of Little Jehanne of France)* — a simultaneous artist's book originally created in watercolours, in which her games with colour and her free geometric constructions accompany rhythmically but without interruptions a poem by Blaise Cendrars. The Delaunays spent their Parisian days frequenting Mondrian and Vantongerloo, in other words, the avant-gardes of Abstraction, and then Pevsner, Gabo, Moholy-Nagy, which means the artists who were quickly and without hesitation proceeding towards Constructivism in sculpture starting from Abstraction. These associations mark the difference or the distance of the couple from Futurism, in search of abstract perspectives, more rigorous in a Modernist sense. Apollinaire attended the exhibitions by the Delaunays, husband and wife.

One day he was very struck by the objects that the two produced and published a review with a very enthusiastic tone: 'You must go to Bullier, on Thursday and on Sunday, M. and M.me Delaunay, who are implementing "the reform of costume." [...] Now here is the description of a simultaneous suit by M.me Sonia Delaunay: violet jacket, long violet and green belt and, under the jacket, a blouse separated into zones of lively, soft or faded colours, mixed in which are antique pink, the colour tango, Nattier blue, scarlet, etc., resultant on various materials, such as linen, taffeta, tulle, plush cotton, iridescent cloth and poult-de-soie juxtaposed. All this variety has not gone unnoticed. It gives fantasy to elegance.'[91]

The years between 1923 and 1934 were of intense and feverish experimentation: Sonia expressed herself through *gouaches* and works in Indian ink or pencil, composing the marvellous pages of her *Black Books*, inventing fabrics, clothes, costumes, objects, scenographic installations and design items starting from many of these drawings, transcending any difference between art, fashion and daily life. The intention was obviously to eliminate the confines, to break with the division between genres to reformulate entire categories. The shifting of concepts and behaviour, of functions and devices, concerned art and architecture, art and fashion above all. Nevertheless,

In the Twenties Sonia Delaunay invented paper fabrics, costumes, objects, scenographic installations and design items, transcending any difference among art, fashion and daily life.
Sonia Delaunay, *Décor géométrique (Geometrical pattern)*, first quarter of the 20th century
Printed crêpe tabby silk fabric, 8.5 x 48 cm
Lyon, Musée des Tissus

Coat created by Sonia Delaunay for Gloria Swanson, by whom Ferragamo came to know the artist's work

Sonia Delaunay, *Décor composé de zig-zag, de carrés (Pattern created by zigzag and squared designs)*, first quarter of the 20th century
Printed crêpe tabby silk fabric, 49 x 20 cm
Lyon, Musée des Tissus

Sonia Delaunay, *Sonia Delaunay: ses peintures, ses objects, ses tissus simultanés, ses modes (Sonia Delaunay: her paintings, her objects, her simultaneous fabrics, her fashion)* (Paris: Librairie des Arts Décoratifs, 1925), plates 1 and 13 (58); 59 (14) Stencils on paper, 56 x 40 cm Florence, Biblioteca Nazionale Centrale. Delaunay's interest in the world of fashion is clear in these illustrations

as Annette Malochet writes: 'The examination of the painting activities of Sonia Delaunay, through the analysis of the *gouaches* contained in the *Black Books* and associated with them, enables us to identify a typology of forms and chromatic systems that then recur in all the rest of her production. Eradicating them from that context, isolating them, the process of perception would be reduced to a simple action of vision. The *Black Books* are personal testimony "in colour" of the designs of Sonia Delaunay and invite us to look deeper and distinguish the motivations and procedures of a behaviour that, even when it enters in the field of fashion or entertainment, does not forget its initial

matrix. They accompany us, like Ariadne's thread, in those ten years of the life of Sonia that were the most troubled and in which her activity as an artist was open to the most diverse experiences, among which that of fashion was not less important.'[92] With this spirit, which never submitted to the demands and attractions of the fashion industry, Sonia Delaunay 'creates, gradually invents and produces costumes for the theatre or non "standardised" clothes for beautiful, wealthy clients such as Gloria Swanson (for whom Ferragamo was to make shoes), Lucienne Bogaert, who filmed *Trohuadec* and *Le coup du 2 décembre*, or for Paulette Pax in *Pygmalion*. Once Sonia summarised her aims and said: 'In 1923 I was contacted by a House from Lyon that was interested in my fabric designs. I also executed 50 designs-colour relations with geometric, rhythmic forms. For me these were and remained ranges of colours, the basis, after all, of the essential concept of our painting (Robert's and my own). All this involved research and many studies. My research was extremely pictorial and was plastically a discovery that was later useful to both for our painting. The rhythm is based on numbers, because colour can be measured against the quantity of vibrations. This is a wholly new conception, which opens up endless horizons for painting and can be employed by whoever feels it and will understand it. After overcoming this stage in my research, which was never theoretical, but only based on sensibility (for me), I acquired a freedom of expression that can be found in my latest works, especially in the *gouaches*, which are expressions of moods, poems.'[93]

THIS IS TOMORROW

Before his death in 1960, Salvatore Ferragamo also had the opportunity to recognise the signs of a new avant-garde, imposed at world level after the historical one of the first half of the century. The beginning of contemporary art coincides for example with exhibitions such as *The Movement* at the Galerie Denise René in Paris, which announced the success of Kinetic art or *This is Tomorrow* in London, focusing on the relationships between art, science, technology, design and popular culture. The Western world, emerging from the terrible tragedy of the Second World War, entered the euphoric phase of consumerism, the conquest of space and new telecommunications. Art became fashionable and fashion dragged every form of artistic expression into its orbit, instantly reproducing what had been experimented with and proposed in the avant-garde galleries. Pop art colours invaded the world of fashion and design, the acid and psychedelic ones of mass production and advertising entered the museums.

The difference between high and low culture, between luxury and mass consumption, thanks to the domination of kitsch, tended entirely to disappear.

The history of art, between the late Fifties and early Sixties, was marked, however, by the appearance on the scene of Pop images (beer cans, advertising, comic strip heroes, Brillo boxes, bottles of Coca-Cola, living or dead icons of cinema and politics), by specific objects, by environment and performance, by poor materials and then by a succession of '-isms' before the domination of kitsch, the ultra-genre that imposed Post-Modernism on the Modernism of the first half of the 20th century. These were years dominated by the immanent yet 'ethereal' figure of Andy Warhol, who after Duchamp imposed a newly conceptual change in art and contemporary communication. Warhol's career began at the Institute of Technology in Pittsburgh, where he studied advertising graphics; in 1949 the young artist settled in New York and immediately came into contact with magazines such as *Harper's Bazaar, Vogue* and *Glamour*, interested as he was in shuffling his cards and reproducing the commercial reality that surrounded him. These were the years of his first artistic tests; he perfected the technique of the *bottled line* and produced images connected with the world of fashion (in which his aesthetic principles, mainly based on the modern notion of kitsch, started to emerge). He created samples of shoes for the

magazines and in 1955 illustrated *A la Recherche du Shoe Perdu* together with Ralph Pomeroy, the author of the texts. In 1956 he exhibited in a group show at the Museum of Modern Art in New York, presenting images of shoes made by collage and decorated with the application of gold leaf. This sumptuous transfiguration of a commercial product, presented in fairytale terms, to enchant and make us believe in a civilisation of consumption as a princely kingdom close at hand, went all around the world. The overturning by Warhol of high values—noble, sacred and aristocratic—and commercial-media fetishism, was just at the beginning. With the Sixties came the burgeoning of the phenomenon of Pop Art, of which Warhol was to be one of the main protagonists, together with Claes Oldenburg, Jim Dine, Roy Lichtenstein, James Rosenquist and Robert Indiana. With Pop Art the difference between high culture and popular culture, between luxury object and commercial product, no longer existed.

Like the other Pop artists, Warhol also overturned the concept of traditional iconography, adjusting it to contemporary life, to its myths, to the global dimensions of mass culture, to the notion of *consumption* as *cannibalism*. The subjects of his paintings (in reality, photo-silkscreened prints on which the painter's manual intervention was reduced to a minimum or was entirely absent) were those that invaded the streets and supermarkets of the Fifties and Sixties, the same that at the time were spread with television: bottles of Coca-Cola, cans of Campbell's soup and Kellogg's cereal boxes, the faces of movie stars (Marilyn Monroe or Liz Taylor), those of dictators and revolutionaries (Mao Zedong and Che Guevara), the symbols of the Capitalist West ($) and of the Socialist utopia (hammer and sickle), icons like Jackie Kennedy and Elvis Presley, Mickey Mouse, flowers, knives, skull and crossbones, electric chairs, road traffic accidents, images of clashes between police and demonstrators. A kind of chaotic place, a collective, Postmodern *vanitas*. Everything that contemporary capitalism 'valued' and presented on the market was embodied by Warhol and transformed into cold simulacrum. He operated with indifference, on the verge of machine-like insensitivity. With his creative cynicism, Warhol marked the end of art, producing a new one, defined by some (for instance by Arthur Danto) as post-historical and post-narrative; that is, dominated by a completely unprecedented relationship between art, market, cultural institutions and mass communication. In other words, placing art and reality in a more foul and vicious circle than the previous one (which, for example, was highlighted by W. Benjamin, especially in the texts devoted to Baudelaire, to fashion and the reproducibility of art), and increasing the reproduction and consumption

Sonia Delaunay, illustrations for the book *Juste présent* by Tristan Tzara (Paris: Fequet et Baudier, 1961) Etching on paper, 30 x 42 cm Florence, Biblioteca Nazionale Centrale

of iconic memory (everything happens in a present without history), Warhol envisaged the art of Postmodern simulacra, pre-announcing and exorcising the ephemeral from fashion, the drift of aesthetic consumerism, from which his operation was detached, imposing itself rather as shadow (in mourning) of the Classical in art. Only Warhol was able in fact to paint a pair of gilded shoes as though they were two figures of Byzantine saints, or to give the portrait of a famous actress the aura of a Madonna by Raphael. 'The perspective is that of indifference. The one-of product was replaced by the repeated work [...] with icy joy,' wrote Achille Bonito Oliva.[94] On the other hand, Warhol had declared that he was and painted like a machine: 'Everything resembles everything else and acts in the same way, with each passing day. I think that all should be machines. I think that everyone should love themselves. Pop art is loving things. Loving things means being like a machine, because it continually does the same thing. I paint in this way because I want to be a machine.'

LUCIO FONTANA. CHILD PRODIGY

Fascinated by the aesthetics of the Baroque, a period in which in his view the figures abandoned the plane of representation to continue living in space, Lucio Fontana drew the epistemological idea of an endless and open spatiality. Immediately the artist sought to free the plastic structure from any adherence to natural truth. In this liberatory process of his, Fontana used the most disparate materials, always seeking an elegance of surfaces that he did not hesitate to find with varnishes and bright colours, already industrial, for design objects; or else with older techniques, Medieval, Romantic or Art Deco (enamelled terracotta, gilded or mosaic plaster). In the early Thirties, Fontana moved towards abstraction and joined the *Abstraction-Création* movement. In 1935 he took part in the first group exhibition of abstract art in Turin, and in the same year his first one man show was held at the Galleria del Milione in Milan, where, among others, Kandinsky and Melotti exhibited. At the same time he applied himself to ceramics in Albissola and Sèvres, an activity that was to lead him to achieve extraordinary results, in a dialogue at a distance with ancient art and with Picasso, with the Informel artists of the first half of the 20th century or with personalities such as Gio Ponti. Especially in ceramics, Fontana 'had fun' evoking ancient myths and stories, to create a ménagerie of real or imaginary creatures (Medusa) and also religious themes (the *Via Crucis*, the *Deposizione* for Milan Cathedral, for example). After the most radical phase of his 'spatialism', Lucio Fontana carried forward a kind of 'childish regression'. The theme of the

Lucio Fontana at work in 1964

golden age and the regression to childhood had been tackled ever since the early 20th century; we need only consider *Fanciullo prodigio* by Carlo Carrà, a canvas from 1915, or certain pages of criticism by Alberto Savinio, of interest for scribbles, for the destruction of objects, for the 'scatology' of many artists starting with Jean Dubuffet (1901–1985). Yet it was Charles Baudelaire who began the comparison between genius and child, considering the topic in *Le peintre de la vie moderne*, a text of fundamental importance for the artistic culture of the 19th century and the early 20th. On those pages Baudelaire associates the inspiration of genius with childhood and that type of sensitivity with convalescence, because he affirms that in the condition of overexcitement, as is that of the child, the perception of the world is open to sensations of unprecedented objectivity. Genius, says Baudelaire, is nothing but '*childhood found again* through an act of will, a childhood provided at this point, to express itself, with virile organs and the analytical spirit that enables him to order the series of materials accumulated in an involuntary process. And it is to this deep and cheerful curiosity that the fixed and animally ecstatic eye of

Jean Vaughan   andy Warhol

Jewel Sans   andy Warhol

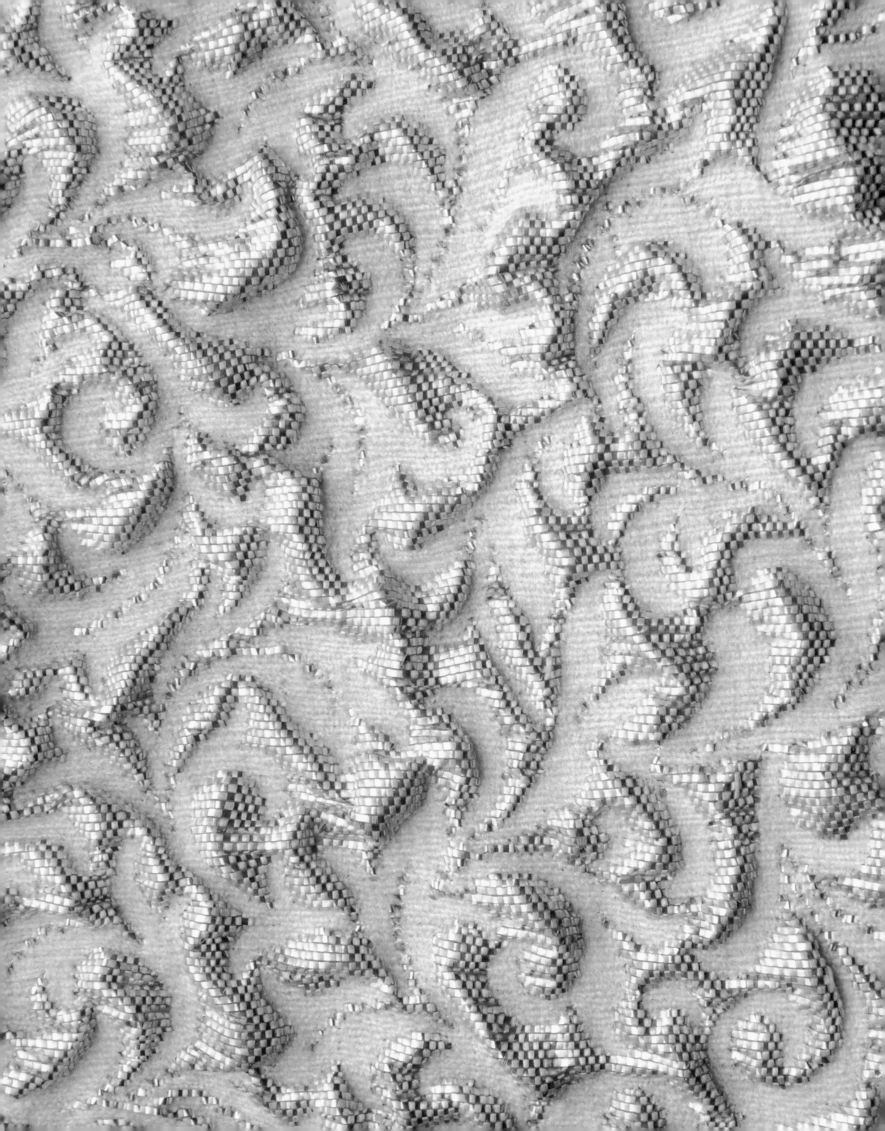

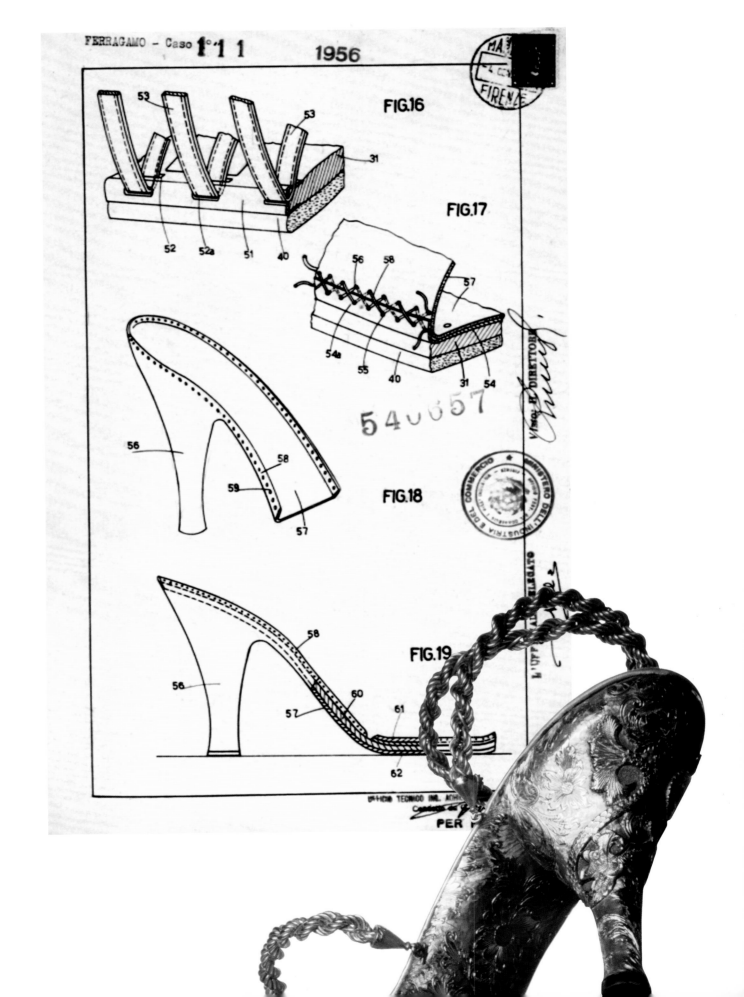

FIG.16

FIG.17

FIG.18

FIG.19

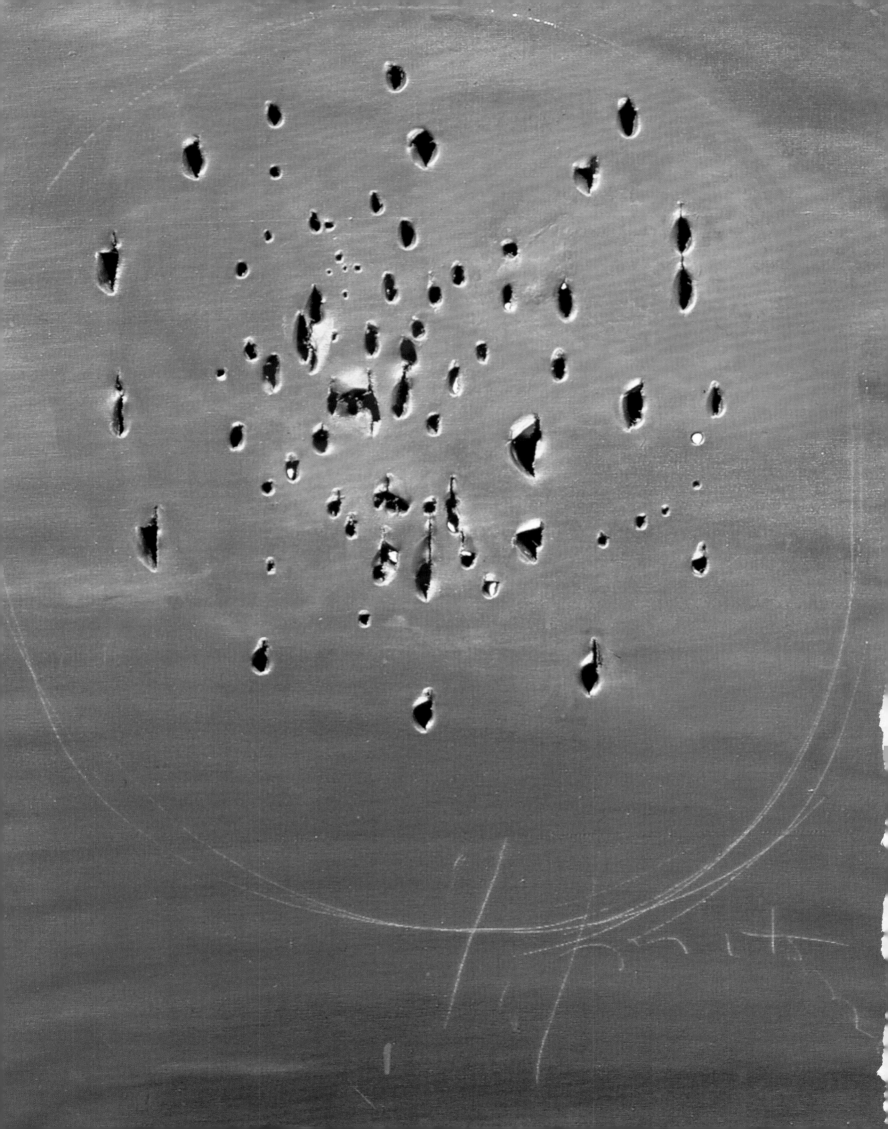

Salvatore Ferragamo, *Damigella*, 1955, prototype for an ankle boot in elasticised silk brocade created for Sophia Loren. Florence, Salvatore Ferragamo Museum

Sano di Pietro, *Madonna con Bambino (Madonna with Child)*, 15th century, tempera on wood. Prato, Farsettiarte Collection

Andy Warhol, *Jean Vaughan (Golden shoe)*, 1956, gold leaf, ink, printed gold collage on paper. Venice, Luigino Rossi Collection

Andy Warhol, *David Evins (Golden shoe)*, 1956, gold leaf, ink, printed gold collage on paper. Venice, Luigino Rossi Collection

Salvatore Ferragamo, *Sandal*, 1956, 18-carat gold upper. Florence, Salvatore Ferragamo Museum

Lucio Fontana, *Concetto spaziale (Spatial concept)*, 1964, oil, graffiti on canvas, gold. Florence, Tornabuoni Arte Collection

Salvatore Ferragamo, *Footwear bottom-stock construction with heel, metal plantar arch and flexible sole*, patent no. 546657, July 28th 1956.
Rome, Archivio Centrale dello Stato

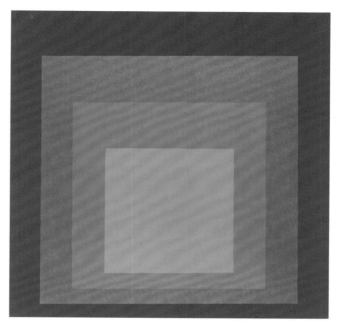

children when faced with the new must be attributed, whatever it is, face or landscape, golden light, colours, iridescent cloth, magic of beauty embellished in the powder room.'[95] For Baudelaire inspiration is something superhuman, possible in a condition of perennial infantilism, provided that the fury is accompanied by great discipline. In short, even to cut a canvas, as in the case of Lucio Fontana, a surgeon's hand is needed. Returning to Fontana, let us recall that his aim was to impose 'a new playful change on his hunger for *kitsch*: from false precious stones glued onto punctured cloth (often painted in the sweet sickly tones of icing for cakes) of the series of "stones" from 1951–58, to the sparkling of diamond powder and the acidic colours (caramel pink and apple green) of the ovals of the series *La fine di Dio* from 1963–64—not to mention the gold coloured paintings—Fontana never stopped declaring [...] that in the middle of late capitalism the only morally sustainable position is that of the irresponsibility of the child who discovers the sparkling variety of a bazaar.'[96] The recourse to precious metals in certain works with a theological theme serves to add (symbolically) an eternal value to the subject of mourning (the death of God) considering that since antiquity the golden colour has been used to 'spatialise' transcendent reality, the infinite. The serious, philosophical side coexisted with the affabulatory and the playful in *La fine di Dio*. Also in this case Fontana moves close to kitsch, without however being totally contaminated by that genre of popular humour. The symbolic dematerialisation of gilding seems to be reduced, in fact, to the manifestation of an elitist taste, to an attraction piloted towards a form of cultural aristocracy, rather than to a form of spiritual adhesion in one form or another. Following the line of the marvel and the child's game, that of drunkenness and aesthetic intoxication which, from the mid-19th century, arrived as far as the Sixties, passing first through the 'alcoholic' Paris of Apollinaire and the Dada cabarets of Zurich and Berlin, let us remember that Lucio Fontana extended his interests to television, to fashion (he designed jewels and provided materials for photographic sets), to the decoration of places of entertainment, introducing, together with his typical figurative motifs, 'neon tubes and Wood lights.'[97]

MATERIALS, COLOURS, UTOPIAS

The world of design (Italian, European and then American) certainly provided motifs of inspiration for Ferragamo. We wish to restrict ourselves here to the designs of the first Bauhaus and then to the research and production of the New Bauhaus (consider for example *Spiral* by Lázló Moholy-Nagy from 1945 in

Joseph Albers, *Homage to the square: delicate perfume*, 1965 Oil on canvas, 60 x 60 cm Hamburg, Hamburger Kunsthalle

Salvatore Ferragamo, *Lucenzia*, 1966, velvet boot made for Brigitte Bardot Florence, Salvatore Ferragamo Museum

relation to his invisible or transparent shoes,[98] and also the research by Josef Albers into colour, the *Variations* from 1947–55 and the *Homages to the Square* executed starting from 1950, regarding the research into colours conducted by Ferragamo).[99] The artists and designers of Bauhaus made possible the marriage of pragmatism and utopia, characterising in this way the experimentation, the popularisation and even the marketing of products, an aesthetic vision that has been extended from architecture to the applied arts, from industrial design to craftsmanship. In one of his *Vorkurs*, Moholy-Nagy explained enthusiastically his conception of 'whole man' and the need to integrate physical, psychic and technological factors: 'Today we are faced with nothing less than the regaining of the biological bases of human life. Only by returning to these can we achieve the maximum use of technical progress in the fields of physical culture, of nutrition, of habitation and industry—a radical reorganisation of our entire pattern of life.'[100]

The Institute of Design in Illinois and the Black Mountain

College were among the most important 'academies' of modernity: a crossroads of fertile minds, of clever experimenters who redefined, together with the fundamental philosophical and aesthetic principles of art and design, also the very way of perceiving music and dance, taste in furnishings and in fashion, the scientific and gestaltic bases of vision and perception. In his courses Josef Albers handled the investigations into form, colour and vision with particular attention, tending to develop manual work, learning through doing. For this, when he arrived in America Albers 'called his preliminary course not *Vorkurs* but *Werklehre*, teaching through work, or teaching by doing. Although the goal remained very similar to that of Bauhaus—"*Werklehre* is a course on materials (for example paper, cardboard, laminate, wire), showing their possibilities and their limitations"—the accent was less on attributing a meaning or a function to a substance and more on inventing a form with it. In his courses Albers used non-traditional materials and objects such as leaves and eggshells, and was interested more in the appearance than in the essence, or rather what he called *matière*, which he defined "as a substance appears" and as it changes with the different manipulations, illuminations and arrangements. This explains his particular obsession for the combination of forms and for the interaction of colours, which he juxtaposed to "show how colours influence and change every other element". "Nothing can be a unique thing, but rather a thousand things", Albers once pointed out; "all art is deception". Part of the visual education concerned the optical illusion and for this reason deception was also a primary interest for Albers in art, in the "discrepancy between the physical fact and the psychic effect".'[101]

FLORENCE THE RISING CITY

Finally Florence. City of *mirabilia* and *naturalia*, of little studios, cloakrooms, of cabinets abounding in precious objects, of masterpieces of lesser art. Florence the place of inspirations and progressive and sudden visions. In the Medici city, Ferragamo found the artisans who were useful to create a new 'company' after those opened in Bonito and in America. He wanted a modern workshop, yet where the work was still organised in a 'traditional' way, in which manual activity and a more spiritual and geometric conception of manufacturing creation still had value. At the same time that 'factory' had to be capable of satisfying the increasingly numerous national and international demands. Then in those streets and in those piazzas, in the churches and in the museums, he found that kind of beauty and harmony that his foreign customers so liked; here he appreciated glimpses

and views of uncontaminated nature between city and countryside. He found an international intellectual and artistic fervour, which perhaps today is wrongly too often undervalued, if not misunderstood. Futurism again marked Florentine culture, after the exploits of the brawl with the Giubbe Rosse and the events at the Teatro Verdi, the first Futurist exhibition in 1913, the birth of *engagé* magazines, the musical evenings, the establishing of a Florentine Modern school that was to include, among others, Primo Conti, the twins Thayaht and Ram, Emilio Notte and Lucio Venna, Antonio Marasco and Marisa Mori, Alberto Magnelli (who very soon left for Paris) and Ottone Rosai; in addition to lively experimentation in architecture, literature and cinema. In 1931 Ferragamo could have visited an exhibition of avant-garde works organised in the Galleria d'Arte Firenze at Via Cavour. That *Mostra futurista. Pittura scultura aeropittura arti decorative architettura* was conceived by Marasco and Thayaht for the Tuscan Futurist Group, and a text by Marinetti was included in the catalogue. Among other things, Thayaht presented three sculptures that may well have struck Ferragamo: *La Bautta, Il Violinista, Il Flautista,* two plasters and one made of white Carrara marble. Resting on the plane, but horizontally, those elegant and musical sculptures seem to recall certain outlines of shoes moulded by Ferragamo in those same years, with an identical perception of the dynamic synthesis of forms and volumes.[102] Two years later, Futurism entered Palazzo Spini Feroni. Between January and February 1933 an exhibition was held of *Arte sacra futurista, aeropittura, pittura e scultura* in the Gallery curated by Luigi Bellini in the building at Via Tornabuoni no. 4. The minds behind the operation were once again Marasco and Thayaht.[103] Intervening in the catalogue was the omnipresent Marinetti, who exalted the room devoted to sacred Futurist art. Marasco had the honour of a personal room. Thayaht was once again surprising. He translated according to timeless codes of elegance the plastic tension of the most typical Futurist monuments, and exhibited an aluminium *Vittoria dell'aria*, with which the artist-designer harkened back, but in reverse, to the reference of the first Marinetti to the Nike of Samothrace, re-evoked here to overcome and annihilate the exaltation of the racing car with an image of a beauty almost superhuman in its spiritual abstraction.[104] In just two years, between 1931 and 1933, in Luigi Bellini's gallery there were exhibitions by de Chirico (perhaps even two), Ottone Rosai and Giovanni Costetti, then one of Rational architecture, in addition to one man shows by Alberto Magnelli, who between 1931 and 1932 had settled definitively in Paris,[105] and by Pietro Annigoni,[106] perhaps met on that very occasion by Ferragamo.

**Alberto Magnelli, *Explosion lirique n. 5. Les Baigneuses (Lyric explosion no. 5. The Bathers)*, 1918
Oil on canvas, 120 x 120 cm
Florence, Private Collection**

THE TIME MACHINE

Florence also offered a vast repertoire of anthropological collections conserved not far from the Uffizi, from Pitti and from the Bargello, from Palazzo Spini Feroni. So we imagine Ferragamo interested in exotic articles, in heterodox shapes, techniques and motifs; a *congerie* of signs now belonging to Western visual culture since the avant-garde (first and foremost Picasso and Matisse, but also Brancusi and Breton, all lovers of primitive and Oriental art, and for this reason keen frequenters of the Musée de l'Homme in Paris) had given aesthetic value to those forms of art, acknowledging the strength of forms and expressive power of those articles, capitalising on what scientists and historians of art had studied of those cultures and of those societies since the second half of the 19th century. In Florence Ferragamo was therefore able to update his idea of a workshop and *Wunderkammer*, in tune with what happened in the studios of artists, in the minds of poets and writers, both of the city and not. This need for visions, for temporal leaps, will undoubtedly have convinced him to engage in an association with Alvaro Monnini, an artist who organised on an abstract base a figurative narration founded on the revival of certain myths at the heart of Italian and Tuscan painting in particular. In addition to Ferragamo, for whom he designed magnificent scarves, Monnini had professional relationships with Oleg Cassini, Emilio Pucci, and with companies such as Valditevere, in a period in which Italian fashion had found in the White Room of Palazzo Pitti in Florence an international launchpad. For Emilio Pucci, for example, Monnini created successful subjects for silk scarves inspired by the Palio in Siena or by famous Florentine paintings, such as Botticelli's *Primavera* and *La battaglia di San Romano* by Paolo Uccello.

Therefore, Ferragamo had a particular predisposition for travelling in time, through different ages and civilisations. On the other hand, the stylist had worked in Santa Barbara and in Hollywood, where visual, literary and also architectural eclecticism were at home. Frequenting those film sets and those studios, he'll have experienced the unhinging of time and space created with sets, shots and montages, an experience of mental travel similar to that of the time machine, a form of exploration of the mythical and the epic, the fantastic and the primordial, resolved by the magic of film and the big screen. The master scenographers of the colossals reconstructed in the various production sites (Universal, Warner Brothers, Fox, Metro Goldwyn Mayer) environments from periods distant in time and in space, and the young Italian shoemaker quickly learned to travel *à rebour* to harmonise his inventions with the costumes used by the stars of the silent movies. In this way, after Hollywood, his time machine became Florence: the kaleidoscope city, the merry-go-round of museums and collections. An open-air live set, day after day. Perhaps, in Florence, he found interesting the collections of Frederick Stibbert (where he was subject to the attractions of Oriental clothing, armour, handwork of various kinds), the archaeological ones and those in progress and *in itinere* at the Natural History Museum (including 'La Specola' and the Anthropology and Ethnology Section, in Palazzo Nonfinito since 1924), collections that from the beginning (at least from the time, that is, of the foundation of the Imperial and Royal Museum of Physical and Natural History) were not destined for the exaltation of the Florentine *genius loci* (lesser arts, archaeology), but for the documentation of the cultures and customs of people from all over the known world, organised encyclopaedically according to scientific and methodological criteria belonging to the various ages. A heritage of demo-ethno-anthropological

**Alvaro Monnini,
*XI Composizione
(XI Composition)*, 1950
Oil on canvas, 156 x 115 cm
Milan, Claudio Monnini
Collection**

***Palazzo*, 1950, printed silk
scarf, 90 x 90 cm, produced
by Salvatore Ferragamo based
on a design by Alvaro Monnini,
signed
Florence, Salvatore Ferragamo
Museum**

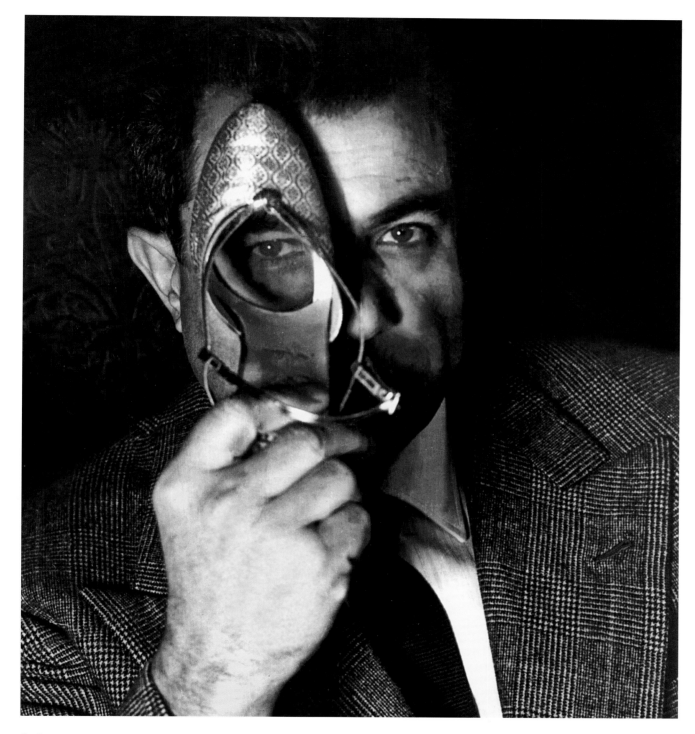

Salvatore Ferragamo looks
through the vinyl sole
of one of his sandals, 1955

finds mostly donated by the greatest explorers and
scientists of the modern age: starting with precious
objects received as gifts from the Medici, such as the
mantle of the Tupinamba, already listed in the inventory
of the armoury of Ferdinand II in 1631. An item of
clothing woven with feathers of *Ibis rubra* ('a simar
of Indian-style red feathers'), which was worn by the
priests of the Sun god on the occasion of rites and
sacred ceremonies. Ferragamo felt a kind of initiatic
dizziness, a visionary drunkenness, similar to what he
had felt at the studios in Hollywood, places that he said

were kaleidoscopic, alienating, electrifying, magical.
And so between America and Italy reminiscences were
mixed with inspirations, visions and evocations that
enabled him magically to participate in many other lives,
projecting him into places and periods more or less
distant or remote. His work would continue after his
death, of this he was sure: 'I have plenty of time.
I know I am going to do it. If it is not done with this
body, it will be done with another. We are all flowing
with the eternal tide, and of the eternal tide only
is there no end.'[107]

1 I. Calvino, *Six Memos for the Next Millennium* (Harvard: Harvard University Press, 1988), p. 81.

2 I am referring to a philosophy that over the centuries has expressed very different ideas from those of modern scientists, who, following the most recent discoveries in the genetics field, think themselves able to explain metempsychosis on scientific bases. The transmission of culture is supposedly a question of DNA. On this issue, cf. L. Cavalli Sforza, *L'evoluzione della cultura* (Turin: Codice Edizioni, 2004).

3 Cf. R. Guénon, 'Mestieri antichi e industria moderna,' in Id., *Il Regno della Quantità e i Segni dei Tempi* (Milan: Adelphi, 1982), pp. 59–64. To explain the difference between quantitative learning and qualitative initiation in the opposing domains of modern industry and traditional activities, Guénon cites 'the notion of *swadharma* as it is understood in Hindu doctrine. The notion is in itself wholly qualitative, as it concerns the carrying out by each being of an activity conforming to their essence or to their nature, and for this reason eminently in conformity with order (*rita*).'

4 Ivi, p. 61.

5 *Ibidem*.

6 *Ibidem*.

7 *Ibidem*.

8 Ivi, p. 62.

9 S. Ferragamo, *Shoemaker of Dreams* (original edition London: George G. Harray & Co., Ltd, 1957; Livorno: Sillabe, 2006), p. 60.

10 Reminiscence is explained by Plato in *Meno*. According to the Athenian philosopher, the soul is immortal and is born and reborn many times therefore; it has seen everything both here and on the other side, and on a given occasion can remember what it already knew beforehand, what it has experienced in a previous life. Thus 'nothing prevents someone who remembers a single thing (which is what is called learning) from finding all the rest by himself, if he has courage and does not tire in the search, since seeking and learning are nothing but reminiscence, since all nature is of the same kind and the soul has learned everything,' in Plato, *Tutti gli scritti*, edited by G. Reale (Milan: Rusconi, 1991), pp. 949–950.

11 S. Ferragamo, *op. cit.*, p. 59.

12 Ivi, pp. 59–60: 'I was born to be a shoemaker, but from whence does my knowledge come? It is not inherited. In late years I searched the records of my ancestors through four hundred years. There was no shoemaker among them. I found many humble property owners, I found a poet, I even found an alchemist; but not shoemaker, not one. Nor have I had to learn in the accepted sense. From my first days with shoes—yes, even with the little white shoes I made for my sisters—I have remembered all about shoemaking. I have remembered: that is the only way to describe it. I have only to sit down and think, and the answers come to me out off the memory of days—it can be only this—when in some previous existence upon this earth I was a shoemaker. There can be no other explanation? How else can I account for the fact that at the age of ten I was a better shoemaker than my master Luigi Festa was at thirty, or at sixty for that matter? How else was it possible for me to learn everything they could teach me in two weeks in that shop in Naples? How else can I explain my sense of design? I do not have to search for styles. When I need new ones, I select from those that present themselves to my mind, as I select an apple from the laden dish upon my table. I read books on astronomy, agriculture, science and chemistry, but never books on shoes and shoemaking. Sometimes I will pick up a copy of *Vogue* or *Harper's Bazaar* and glance at the dresses because I am interested in the general trends of fashion; but when I come to a section on shoes I flick over without bothering to read. Yet I can sit down at my work-table tomorrow and design shoes wich will not resemble any I have invented in the past, and I have invented many. [...] Today, now that I can reflect and ponder, I have come to a belief in the reincarnation of Man in his evolution towards perfection. It seems to me that though my ideas are born out of the past, yet they reach me perfected. They come to me full-blown on the cosmic tide, all ancient errors smoothed away. I remember vividly my first experience of this "memory returning".'

13 This is the title of a publication by E. Zolla, *Verità segrete esposte in evidenza. Sincretismo e fantasia. Contemplazione ed esotericità* (Venice: Marsilio, 1990).

14 S. Ferragamo, *op. cit.*, p. 239.

15 R. Guénon, *op. cit.*, p. 61.

16 S. Ferragamo, *op. cit.*, p. 59.

17 For example in S. Ferragamo, *op. cit.*, pp. 100–101 and in particular p. 124.

18 R. Guénon, *op. cit.*, p. 59.

19 S. Ferragamo, *op. cit.*, p. 69.

20 Ivi, pp. 67–69.

21 Ferragamo often met people tormented by serious orthopaedic problems and with compromised psychological conditions, for example the wife of an important public official in Florence whose 'temper was uncontrollable.' So Ferragamo advised that official to let a physician friend see the lady; after the visit, he gave his professional response: 'Salvatore, I am afraid, her mind is slightly unbalanced.' But it did not end there. Some time went by and the couple entered the shop and Ferragamo had the opportunity to check the woman's feet before building a beautiful pair of shoes to fit her perfectly. 'A few weeks later'—the stylist writes—'the husband came to me in awe and wonder: "What have you done to my wife?" he asked. "She is a different woman!" How many times has that happened! Husbands and sweethearts, sons and brothers—more often than the women themselves—have come to my salon and said those words: "What have you done to her? She is a different woman!" Within the last two or three years, two specialists have sent me mental cases. A few weeks ago—while I was engaged on the writing on this book—I met one of them in Naples. He said: "What did you do to that woman I sent you?" I said: "I made her some shoes". "How is she?" "She is fine!", he said. "She has lost her hallucinations"; ivi, pp. 159–160.

22 Ivi, p. 193.

23 In the same year of the publication of this important theoretical text, Severini was working in Tuscany, in the castle of Montefugoni, where he frescoed a room with figures of Pulcinella and Harlequin.

24 G. Severini, *Dal cubismo al classicismo, estetica del numero e del compasso*, edited by E. Pontiggia (Milan: SE Editore, 1997), p. 17.

25 *Ibidem*.

26 Ivi, p. 22.

27 Ivi, p. 27.

28 Ivi, p. 31.

29 Ivi, p. 34.

30 *Ibidem*.

31 *Ibidem*.

32 *Ibidem*.

33 Ivi, p. 47.

34 S. Ferragamo, *op. cit.*, pp. 52, 87.

35 *Ibidem*.

36 Ivi, p. 60.

37 Ivi, p. 85.

38 Ivi, pp. 138–139.

39 Ivi, p. 141.

40 Ivi, pp. 206–208. On Greta Garbo and Salvatore Ferragamo, see *Greta Garbo. The Mystery of Style,* catalogue for the exhibition, edited by S. Ricci (Milan: Skira, 2010).

41 Indeed Krishnamurti was to visit Florence again after the Sixties, but this is of no concern to our research here.

42 Vanda Scaravelli also had met and listened to Krishnamurti in Holland in 1929, subsequently remaining in contact with him and meeting him on several occasions in Switzerland and in India.

43 G. Polizzi, 'Interview with E. Garin', in 'Filosofia del linguaggio: prospettive di ricerca,' in *Humana Mente*, no. 4, February 2008, p. 212.

44 Arturo Reghini usually signed his articles using pseudonyms, especially in the period when the Fascists were hostile to his ideas.

45 E. Zolla, 'Arturo Reghini', in *Uscite dal mondo* (Milan: Adelphi, 1995), pp. 446–447.

46 *Leonardo* was founded by Giovanni Papini and Giuseppe Prezzolini, together with Giovanni Costetti, Adolfo De Carolis and others and was published by Vallecchi of Florence between 1903 and 1907.

47 Cf. G. Lista, who writes: 'Occultism and phenomenics concern psychic phenomena and met with great success. The terrain was prepared by the writers of Scapigliatura, such as Emilio Praga and Igino Ugo Tarchetti, whose works displayed a certain fascination. In the wake of Edgar Allan Poe, for the invisible, the strange, the fantastic [...] Gabriele D'Annunzio allowed himself to be tempted by occultism. [...] The supporters of Melena P. Blavatsky created Theosophical societies in Bologna, Florence, Milan and Rome [...] while the images of ectoplasms associated with what is called "transcendental photography" became an iconographic genre recognised by the scholars tackling phenomena of mediums, magnetic radiation and materialisations. New societies were born [...] Occultism, esoterism, spiritualism, Theosophy, Buddhism, Oriental religions and "Indian philosophy" are the necessary antidotes for those who want to challenge the materialism of positivist culture'; in *Futurismo. La rivolta dell'avanguardia / Die Revolte der Avantgarde* (Cinisello Balsamo: Silvana Editoriale, 2008), p. 52.

48 Ivi, p. 60.

49 Ivi, pp. 60–62.

50 Ivi, p. 62.

51 This was the case of Luigi Pirandello, who was to refer to spiritualism and psychism on a number of occasions, through the characters of his theatre, his novels, stories and novellas. Significant elements in this regard are to be found in *Il Fu Mattia Pascal* and in *Sei personaggi in cerca di autore*, not to mention *I giganti della montagna,* originally entitled *I fantasmi*. The Sicilian writer was to polemicise with the philosopher Benedetto Croce over this, wishing to defend the inexplicable processes of artistic creation from mechanism, and in order to give scientific substance to his thought he cited the experiments of Alfred Binet—those described in the book *Les altérations de la personalité*, 1892—'through which the presumed unity of the self was reduced to a temporary aggregate, divisible and modifiable, of various more or less clear states of awareness.' Pirandello's characters and masks live in relation to an 'other' world; they perceive shadows, they recognise

signs of elsewhere, they feel that this life is not the only one and that reality is not only the visible one. As Macchia writes, in 'Luigi Pirandello,' in *Storia della Letteratura Italiana*, edited by E. Cecchi and N. Sapegno, Vol. IX, *Il Novecento* (Milan: Garzanti, 1969), p. 448, Pirandello was a 'great teacher of the shudder, of the phantomatic shudder.' He did not fear, nor did he avoid encountering ghosts and presences from another life. 'He had a habitual relationship [...] with the mysteries of reincarnation. Through nightmares, dreams, obsessions, images, meditations, also the feeling of another existence was not unknown to him'; ivi, pp. 453, 485.

[52] The film by Arnaldo Ginna has been lost; only a few images and a few frames have survived, among which *The dance of geometric splendour*.

[53] G. Lista, *Futurismo. La rivolta...* cit., p.122.

[54] Ivi, p. 124 and p. 280.

[55] *Ibidem*. Lista describes a widespread situation: 'In Ferrara, where the painter of the mystical awakening, Gaetano Previati, was born, the poets Corrado Covoni and Filippo de Pisis were passionate enthusiasts of magic and esoterism; in Bologna, Piero Illari and Athos Cesarini were interested in Theosophy and metapsychic research; in Mantua, Gino Cantarelli was to create abstract designed inspired by "medianic visions," etc...'

[56] M. Fidolini, *Dal secondo futurismo al cartellone pubblicitario* (Bologna: Grafis Edizioni, 1987), p. 93.

[57] M. Pratesi, '1920. Thayaht inventa la Tuta e nasce il Made in Italy,' in *Thayaht. Un artista alle origini del Made in Italy*, exhibition catalogue (Prato, Textile Museum, December 15th 2007 – April 14th 2008), (Prato: Museo del Tessuto Edizioni, 2007), p. 17. The whole essay by Pratesi is of considerable interest and offers starting points for a parallel with Ferragamo. The suggestions regarding Kandinsky, Art Deco and Johannes Itten are important, cf. in particular pp.17–20.

[58] Ivi, p. 18.

[59] *Ibidem*.

[60] *Ibidem*.

[61] *Ibidem*.

[62] *Ibidem*.

[63] Ivi, pp. 18–19.

[64] Ivi, p. 19.

[65] Rimbaud confessed that he loved 'idiotic paintings, transom lights, decorations, acrobats' cloths, insignias, popular images; old-fashioned literature, church Latin, erotic books without words, novels of great grandmothers, stories of fairies, books for children, old works, naive refrains, simple rhythms.' To this atlas of emotions, he adds other revolutionary imaginations: 'I dreamed of crusades, voyages of discovery of which no reports exists, republics without history, repressed wars of religion, revolutions of custom, migrations of races and continents: I believed in all enchantments.' Rimbaud says that the world is unprecedented, everything to be discovered, and life offers continuous opportunities for enchantment. He reawakens dulled levels of knowledge.

[66] S. Ferragamo, *op. cit.*, p. 227.

[67] In G. Barche, 'Alfredo Bortoluzzi. "Al freddo" al Bauhaus,' in *Bauhaus 1919–1933. Da Kandinsky a Klee, da Gropius a Mies van der Rohe* (Milan: Mazzotta, 1996), p. 218.

[68] Ivi, p. 219.

[69] G. Lista, *Futurismo. La rivolta...* cit., p. 34.

[70] *Ibidem*.

[71] *Ibidem*.

[72] In V. Gavioli, 'Balla, La vita e l'arte,' in *Balla. I classici dell'arte* (Milan: Skira, 2004), p. 49.

[73] *Ibidem*.

[74] Ivi, p. 50.

[75] *Ibidem*.

[76] E. Princi, 'Materiali Futuristi,' in *Storia dell'Arte Universale*, Vol. 16, *Le Avanguardie* (Milan: Corriere della Sera Education, 2008), p. 175.

[77] Ivi, p. 172.

[78] *Ibidem*.

[79] This was the stage design for the work by Stravinsky *The Song of the Nightingale*, which was not successful for various reasons, among which Depero's simultaneous commitment as costume designer in Picasso's *Parade*.

[80] M. Scudiero, 'Il futurismo trasversale di Fortunato Depero,' in *Depero opere 1914–1953* (Farsettiarte Editore: Milan-Cortina, 2008), p. 13.

[81] Ivi, p. 15.

[82] G. Balla, *Scritti futuristi*, collected and edited by G. Lista (Milan: Abscondita, 2010), p. 66.

[83] The study of photography, particularly the experiments by American Eadweard Muybridge (1830–1904) and the French physiologist Etienne J. Marey (1830–1904), prompted him to represent figures in movement, stressing the theme of dynamism and simultaneity. Scientific interests were fundamental in dealing with experimentation into colour and light, beyond the first Divisionist phase.

[84] G. Lista, *Balla* (Modena: Galleria Fonte d'Abisso, 1982), p. 42.

[85] G. Lista, *Futurismo. La rivolta...* cit., p. 238.

[86] In an interview Balla states that: 'Modern man leans towards colour. This is shown by more or less Parisian fashions. The hats, the parasols, the clothes of our ladies and the handkerchiefs and ties that we wear. And what has Futurist painting actually been from its beginning to today if not a search for abstract chromatic decorativism? And this is because our art is essentially decorative, and today we orientate ourselves towards art applied to industry. This form of art moves us a lot closer to the masses and can be understood and felt by all. In fact in England there are already living rooms futuristically furnished. In Italy there are not. I cannot understand how people of the so-called intellectual world are still able to live in apartments furnished in the unhygienic Rococo style or among the unpleasant gilding in Louis style and can still admire and delight in the tapestries that beatified the gazes of the beautiful Castilians and troubadours of the 15th century. It is the environment that shapes man. In old, dusty rooms, the gnawing of woodworm resonates, and invited to the joys of sweet leisure, we will replace this with vivifying environments, full of lights, of colours, of forms that fit the intensity, the practicality and the dynamism of modern life. In the field of art applied to industry we await a great battle'; in G. Lista, *Balla...* cit., p. 86.

[87] A. Malochet, 'Amare il colore,' in *Sonya Delaunay. Atelier simultané*, edited by A. Malochet, M. Bianchi (Milan: Skira, 2006), p. 20.

[88] Cf. *Le futurisme à Paris, une avant-garde explosive*, edited by Didier Ottinger (Paris: Edition du Centre Georges Pompidou, 2009), p. 288.

[89] On this clash and on the ideological and poetic motivations, read the indispensable study by E. Coen, *Simultanéité, simultanéisme, simultanisme*, ivi, pp. 52–57.

[90] G. Apollinaire, *I pittori cubisti. Meditazioni estetiche*, translation by F. Minoia, with explanatory notes by C. Carrà (Milan: SE Editore, 1996), p. 25.

[91] G. Apollinaire, 'La femme assise,' in *Mercure de France*, 1934, in A. Malochet, *op. cit.*, p. 19.

[92] Ivi, pp. 20–21.

[93] Ivi, pp.17–18.

[94] Achille Bonito Oliva, *Autocritico, automobile* (Rome: Castelvecchi, 2002), p. 109.

[95] 'Convalescence is a return to childhood. The convalescent possesses to a high degree as does a child, the faculty to be warmly interested in things, also those apparently more banal. The child sees everything in the form of a novelty; he is always intoxicated. Nothing resembles so much what we call inspiration as much as the joy with which a child absorbs form and colour. But I would like to go further: I say that inspiration has some relationship with *congestion*, and that every sublime thought is close to a nervous shudder, more or less intense, that has its effect on the brain... But genius is nothing but *childhood found again* through an act of will, a childhood provided at this point, to express itself, with virile organs and the analytical spirit that enables him to order the series of materials accumulated in an involuntary process. And it is to this deep and cheerful curiosity that the fixed and animally ecstatic eye of children when faced with the new must be attributed, whatever it is, face or landscape, golden light, colours, iridescent cloth, magic of beauty embellished in the powder room'; in C. Baudelaire, *Opere*, edited by G. Raboni, G. Montesano, introduction by G. Macchia (Milan: Mondadori, 1996), p. 1280.

[96] H. Foster, R. Krauss et al., *Arte del 1900, Modernismo, Antimodernismo, Postmodernismo* (Bologna: Zanichelli, 2006), p. 413.

[97] *Ibidem*.

[98] In relation to transparent shoes, see also the sculptures of Naum Gabo, for example *Linear Construction in Space no.1* from 1944–45, who already created works in transparent plastic in 1920; on this subject cf. R. Krauss, 'Lo spazio analitico: Futurismo e Costruttivismo,' in *Passaggi, Storia della scultura da Rodin alla Land Art* (Milan: Bruno Mondadori, 1998), pp. 51–77.

[99] Cf. S. Ricci, 'Creatività a colori,' in *Creatività a colori / Creativity in colour*, exhibition catalogue (Florence, Salvatore Ferragamo Museum, December 6th 2006 – April 26th 2010), edited by S. Ricci (Livorno: Sillabe, 2006), pp. 7–13.

[100] In H. Foster, R. Krauss et al., *op. cit.*, p. 344.

[101] Ivi, p. 345.

[102] In that exhibition the works of Ram, Viani, Fillia, Tullio D'Albissola and Farfa were also on display, along with architectural designs by Sant'Elia. On this exhibition and the complete list, and in general on Futurism in Florence and in Tuscany, cf. *Il Futurismo attraverso la Toscana*, edited by E. Crispolti and with essays by E. Crispolti, E. Godoli, D. Lombardi, G. Luti, M. Pratesi and M. Verdone (Cinisello Balsamo: Silvana Editoriale, 2000). On the 1931 Florentine exhibition, in particular pp.108–115.

[103] The list of Tuscan artists, but not only, is long and important: Marisa Mori, Gino Vallecchi, Mario Bandini, Rodolfo Coghei, Vasco Melani, obviously Thayaht and Ram, then Fillia, Diulgheroff, Dottori, Oriani, Prampolini, Saladin, Mino Rosso, Tullio D'Albissola and others besides.

[104] *Il Futurismo attraverso la Toscana...* cit., pp. 116–132.

[105] His *Esplosioni liriche* are from 1918–19.

[106] In addition to those of Sironi, Tosi, Funi, Nomellini, Vagnetti and Griselli. For a more detailed list and further information, *Arte moderna a Firenze, Cataloghi di Esposizioni 1900–1933*, edited by A. Calcagni Abrami and Lucia Chimirri (Florence: Centro Di, 1988), p. 65 and bibliography, p. 72.

[107] S. Ferragamo, *op. cit.*, p. 239.

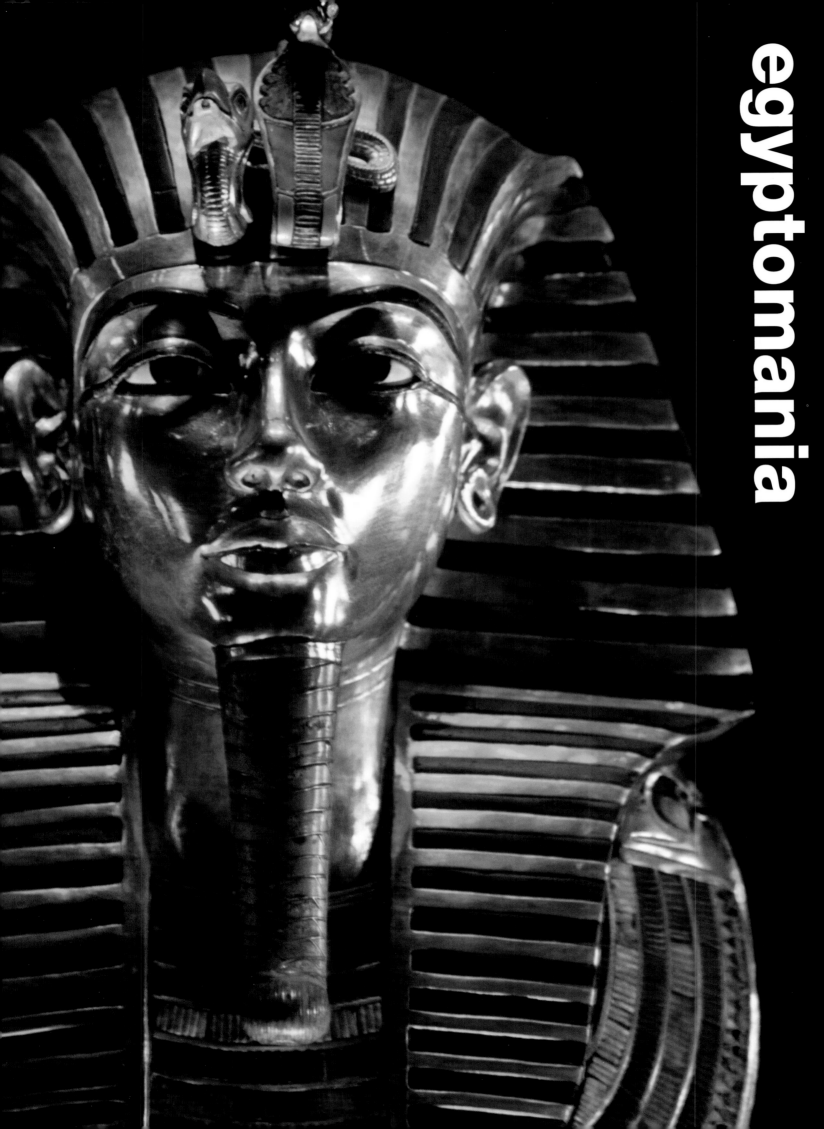

egyptomania

The gold mask of the pharaoh Tutankhamon, found in his tomb in the Twenties and now in the Cairo Museum

The archaeologist Howard Carter opening one of the four caskets that surrounded the sarcophagus of the pharaoh Tutankhamon in the Valley of the Kings, 1922

The reconstruction of some of the articles in Tutankhamon's tomb at the British Empire Exhibition at Wembley in February 1924

The actress Theda Bara in the 1917 film *Cleopatra*, which already reflected the rise of Egyptomania

Salvatore Ferragamo, *Sandal*, 1930, pyramid heel. Florence, Salvatore Ferragamo Museum

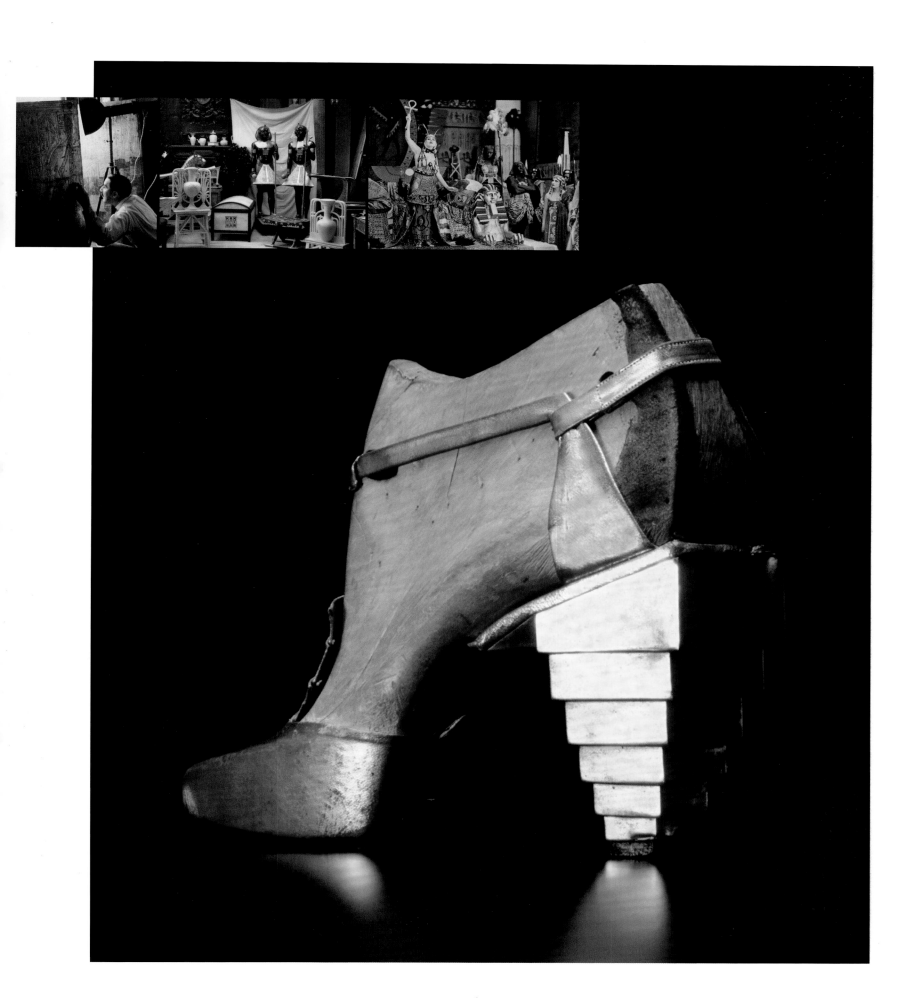

whirls and spirals

Salvatore Ferragamo, *Court shoe*, 1930, kid skin decorated with painted circular decoration. Florence, Salvatore Ferragamo Museum

Roman Art, *Hemispheric bowl*, imperial age, 1st–2nd century AD, glass and mosaic. Florence, National Archaeological Museum

Salvatore Ferragamo, *Court shoe*, 1930, antelope skin decorated with painted circular decoration. Florence, Salvatore Ferragamo Museum

curves and straight lines

Salvatore Ferragamo, *Arcobaleno (Rainbow)*, 1935, court shoe in embroidered suede. Florence, Salvatore Ferragamo Museum

Sonia Delaunay, *Décor de larges bandes ondulantes en noir, en rouge, rose pale, 2 tons de gris (Pattern of large undulated stripes in black, red, pale pink, 2 grey chromatic accents)*, August 1924, printed crêpe tabby silk fabric. Lyon, Musée des Tissus

Roman Art, *Hemispheric bowl*, imperial age, 1st–2nd century AD, glass with stripes in various colours. Florence, National Archaeological Museum

Salvatore Ferragamo, *Sandal*, 1930, kid and grosgrain fabric. Florence, Salvatore Ferragamo Museum

Sample book, third quarter of the 20th century, paper, cardboard; samples of uppers in vegetable and artificial fibres. Signa (Florence), Straw and Weaving Museum 'Domenico Michelacci'

Salvatore Ferragamo, *Sandal*, 1955, upper in Manila straw fabric interwoven with raffia and heel covered with kid. Florence, Salvatore Ferragamo Museum

Salvatore Ferragamo, *Sandal*, 1932, straw. Florence, Salvatore Ferragamo Museum

Sonia Delaunay, *Pois noir sur fond blanc, lignes bleus, cyan, rouges, jaune et vertes (black dots on white back ground with cyan blue, red, yellow and green lines)*, July 1924, printed crêpe tabby silk fabric. Lyon, Musée des Tissus

Salvatore Ferragamo, *Sandal*, 1938–40, raffia with cork wedge heel. Florence, Salvatore Ferragamo Museum

Sonia Delaunay, *Untitled no. 1412* (Paris: Librairie des Arts Décoratifs, 1928), gouache on paper

archaic graphism

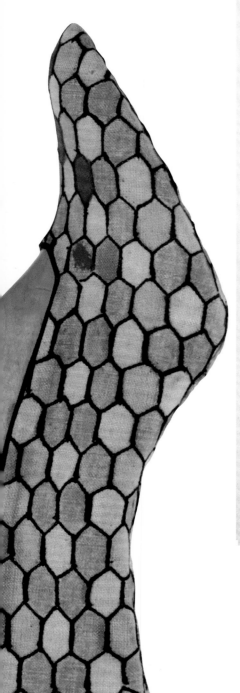

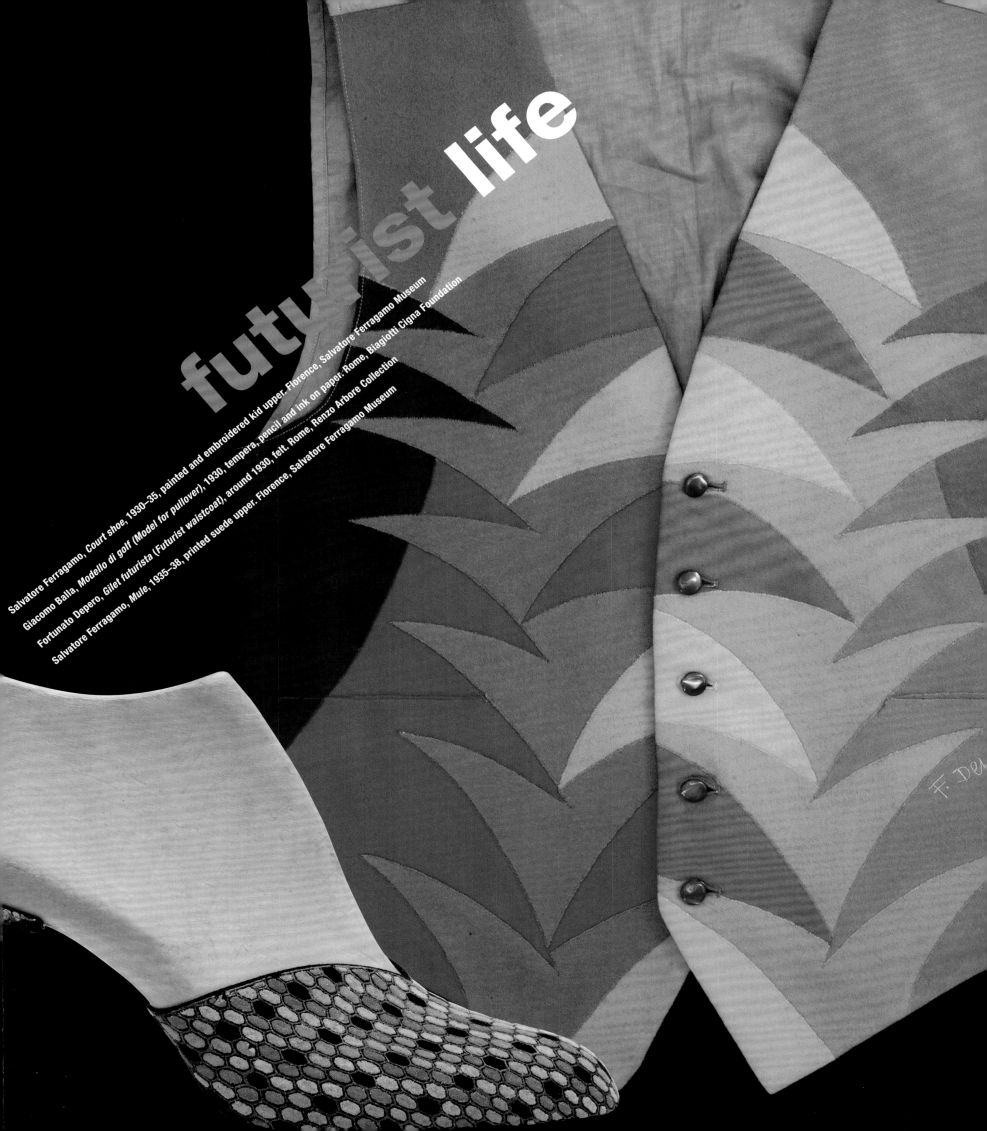

futurist life

Salvatore Ferragamo, *Court shoe*, 1930–35, painted and embroidered kid upper. Florence, Salvatore Ferragamo Museum

Giacomo Balla, *Modello di golf (Model for pullover)*, 1930, tempera, pencil and ink on paper. Rome, Biagiotti Cigna Foundation

Fortunato Depero, *Gilet futurista (Futurist waistcoat)*, around 1930, felt. Rome, Renzo Arbore Collection

Salvatore Ferragamo, *Mule*, 1935–38, printed suede upper. Florence, Salvatore Ferragamo Museum

moving colours

Giacomo Balla, Progetto di ventaglio (Design for a fan), 1918, watercolour and paint on paper. Rome, Biagiotti Cigna Foundation

Salvatore Ferragamo, Laced shoe, 1938, suede upper. Florence, Salvatore Ferragamo Museum

Giacomo Balla, Abito futurista (Futurist suit), around 1920, wool felt. Milan, Ottavio and Rosita Missoni Collection

FUTUR BALLA

patchwork

Sonia Delaunay, *Décor composé de triangles formant une mosaïque (Pattern compounded by triangles making mosaic work)*, first quarter of the 20th century, watered and printed silk crêpe. Lyon, Musée des Tissus

Salvatore Ferragamo, *Fiamma*, 1939, court shoe with patchwork upper in calf and suede. Florence, Salvatore Ferragamo Museum

Salvatore Ferragamo, *Laced shoe*, 1935–38, patchwork upper with embroidered cotton squares. Florence, Salvatore Ferragamo Museum

Giacomo Balla, *Due studi di golf (Two pullover projects)*, 1930, pencil and tempera on paper. Rome, Biagiotti Cigna Foundation

Sonia Delaunay, *Variation sur forme géométriques, base traingle, bleu, blanc, rouge (Changing movement on triangular based geometrical designs coloured with blue, white and red)*, May 1924, printed crêpe tabby silk fabric. Lyon, Musée des Tissus

Salvatore Ferragamo, *Sandal*, 1936, kid and canvas embroidered to create a patchwork effect. Florence, Salvatore Ferragamo Museum

weaves

Sonia Delaunay, *Composition sur la base du carré (Composition based on squared forms)*, first quarter of the 20th century, printed crêpe tabby silk fabric. Lyon, Musée des Tissus

Fortunato Depero, *Elasticità di gatti (Suppleness of Cats)*, 1936–39, oil on canvas. Prato, Farsettiarte Collection

Sonia Delaunay, *Sonia Delaunay: ses peintures, ses objects, ses tissus simultanés, ses modes (Sonia Delaunay: her paintings, her objects, her simultaneous fabrics, her fashion)* (Paris: Librairie des Arts Décoratifs, 1925), stencil on paper. Florence, Biblioteca Nazionale Centrale

Salvatore Ferragamo, *Court shoe*, patent no. 6937, November 27th 1929, lady's shoe with crossed stripes. Rome, Archivio Centrale dello Stato

F. Depero

Domanda N. 306

FRV. IND. N.

L'Ufficiale Delegato

compositions

abstract

Sonia Delaunay, *Décor géométrique basé sur le jéu des rectangles en écru, rouge, gris, et noir (Geometrical pattern based on multicoloured rectangles: ecru, red, grey and black)*, first quarter of the 20th century, printed crêpe tabby silk fabric. Lyon, Musée des Tissus

Salvatore Ferragamo, *Court shoe*, 1930, antelope skin with painted circular decoration. Florence, Salvatore Ferragamo Museum

triangles and rectangles

Sonia Delaunay, *Sonia Delaunay: ses peintures, ses objects, ses tissus simultanés, ses modes (Sonia Delaunay: her paintings, her objects, her simultaneous fabrics, her fashion)* (Paris: Librairie des Arts Décoratifs, 1925), stencils on paper. Florence, Biblioteca Nazionale Centrale

Sonia Delaunay, *Décor composé de chevrons et de rayures (Pattern made by zigzag moulding and stripes)*, first quarter of the 20th century, printed cut velvet silk fabric. Lyon, Musée des Tissus

Salvatore Ferragamo, *Laced shoe*, 1938, suede upper. Florence, Salvatore Ferragamo Museum

geometries and contrasts

Lucio Venna, *Advertising sketch for magazine*, 1928, stencil on paper. Florence, Salvatore Ferragamo Museum

Salvatore Ferragamo, *Court shoe*, 1930, antelope skin decorated with painted circular decoration. Florence, Salvatore Ferragamo Museum

Sonia Delaunay, *Semis de carrés et de rectangles traversés de créneaux (Half-squared and rectangle forms crossed by half lines)*, first quarter of the 20th century

optical

Sonia Delaunay, *Sonia Delaunay: ses peintures, ses objects, ses tissus simultanés, ses modes (Sonia Delaunay: her paintings, her objects, her simultaneous fabrics, her fashion)* (Paris : Librairie des Arts Décoratifs, 1925), stencils on paper. Florence, Biblioteca Nazionale Centrale

Sonia Delaunay, *Décor géométrique (Geometrical pattern)*, first quarter of the 20th century, printed velvet tabby silk. Lyon, Musée des Tissus

Salvatore Ferragamo, *Labirinto (Labyrinth)*, 1927–30, court shoe with embroidered kid upper. Florence, Salvatore Ferragamo Museum

Salvatore Ferragamo, Sandal, 1940, suede upper. Florence, Salvatore Ferragamo Museum | Unknown designer, Parasol, 1920–30, intarsia of Lenci cloth. Gorizia, Musei Provinciali | Giacomo Balla, Motivo per stoffa con linee andamentali (Fabric pattern with moving and leading lines), 1922, tempera and pencil on paper. Rome, Biagiotti Cigna Foundation | Giacomo Balla, Modello per stoffa 'circolanti' (Fabric pattern, circle-lines), 1922, tempera and pencil on paper. Rome, Biagiotti Cigna Foundation

circle-lines

.THAYAHT.
9, Via Dante da Castiglione
FIRENZE, 34 - Italia

blue zig **zag**

Unknown designer, *Parasol*, 1920–30, intarsia of Lenci cloth. Gorizia, Musei Provinciali

Salvatore Ferragamo, *Lady's shoe with vertical thread patterns in different colour tones*, patent no. 6936, November 27th 1929. Rome, Archivio Centrale dello Stato

Salvatore Ferragamo, *Court shoe*, 1930–35, fish skin. Florence, Salvatore Ferragamo Museum

ROTORELIEF N° 8 — CERCEAUX — MODÈLE DÉPOSÉ

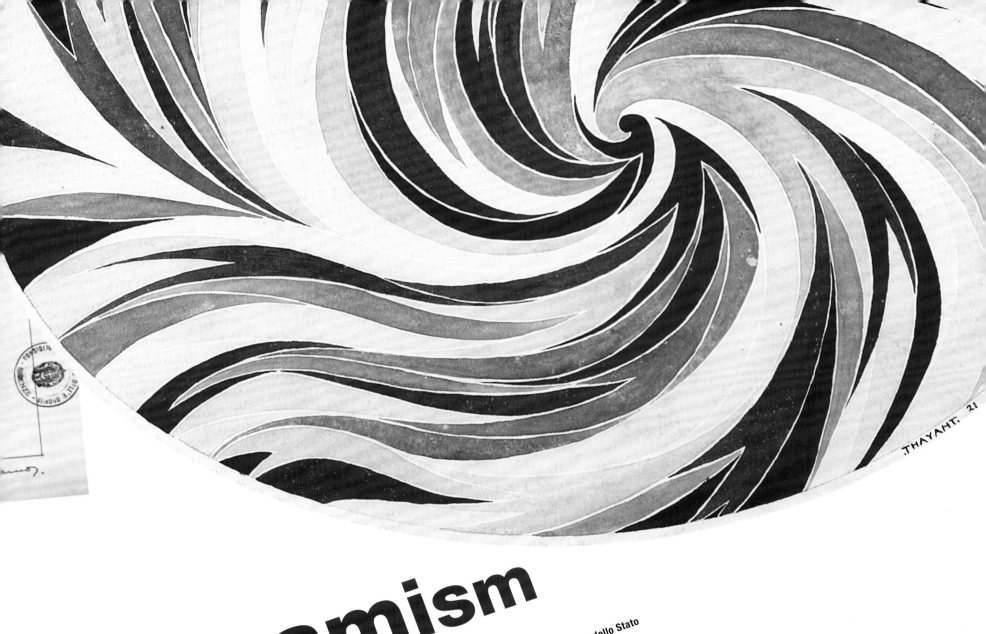

dynamism

Marcel Duchamp, *Rotorelief*, 1936, print on cardboard. Florence, Biblioteca Nazionale Centrale

Salvatore Ferragamo, *Laced shoe*, patent no. 7867, February 21st 1931, boot for women with spiral embroideries. Rome, Archivio Centrale dello Stato

Thayaht, *Vort – motivo decorativo astratto ovale (Vort—oval abstract decorative motif)*, 1921, tempera and pencil on paper. Rome, Private Collection

Salvatore Ferragamo, *Sandal*, 1935–38, suede and Tavarnelle lace. Florence, Salvatore Ferragamo Museum

underwater rhythms

Thayaht, *Pesci (Ritmi subacquei) (Fish—underwater rhythms)*, 1931, oil on wood. Rome, CLM Seeber Collection

Giacomo Balla, *Progetti per scarpe (Designs for shoes)*, 1928–29, pencil and Indian ink on paper. Rome, Biagiotti Cigna Foundation

Società Ceramica Richard-Ginori based on a design by Gio Ponti, *Nautica*, 1927, bowl in polychrome porcelain. Sesto Fiorentino (Florence), Museo Richard-Ginori della Manifattura di Doccia

Sonia Delaunay, *Gros ruban composé de bandes ondulantes (Ribbon pattern created by waves)*, first quarter of the 20th century, printed muslin silk fabric. Lyon, Musée des Tissus

Salvatore Ferragamo, *Court shoe*, 1930–35, upper in embroidered calfskin. Florence, Salvatore Ferragamo Museum

simultaneity

'The good master craftsman lives in a mobile home' IBN KHALDUN

THE GEOMETRIES OF THE SOUL: SALVATORE FERRAGAMO'S TRIUMPHS OF FASHION AND PERCEPTION OF THE ELSEWHERE

LUCA SCARLINI

Right from the beginning of his career, in fact from the time when he was still a child in his ancestral town of Bonito (Avellino), Salvatore Ferragamo always made plain his desire to take care of the body of his customers in particular and of humanity in general, by means of an understanding of the nature and the needs of the foot. In his autobiography *Shoemaker of Dreams* (1957) the leitmotiv is undoubtedly that of the shoe as possibility for the passing on of a benefit, one that is at once physical and spiritual and that spreads rapidly through the whole organism. Among the many stories he tells in it, one about a nephew suffering from poliomyelitis stands out. 'I fitted to the damaged foot a perfect shoe and on the good foot I fitted a shoe so constructed that the moment he put his foot to the ground he complained that I was hurting him [...] The pain in his good foot and the comfort in his crippled one forced him to use the foot he had never expected to use again.'[1] In this sense the creator of futuristic solutions, which stemmed from his personal intuition and the time needs, expressed a very clear vision of his work as a mission.

The determination he showed throughout his existence was, in the first place, not to work with machines (there were few exceptions), but always to remain within the limits of a handicraft world, whose methods the designer wanted to revolutionise but not the spirit, which had to remain that of tradition. At work here was an overriding creative vocation that he had felt since childhood and had to defend fiercely against the opposition of his parents, who did not consider the trade he dreamed of good enough even for someone who came from a family of limited economic means. In the end, after a series of events that in his autobiographical writings take on the character of *exempla*, anecdotes of an exemplary destiny, his thinking found general acceptance. The declaration that he was working for a new wellbeing was linked on the one hand to the search for geometrically daring forms and on the other to the clear perception of a reminiscence of experiences from earlier ages. 'When they had pointed out the work that must be done the knowledge came back as if I had been reminded of a task I had forgotten.'[2] And then, with even greater precision: 'Today, now that I can reflect and ponder, I have come to a belief in the reincarnation of Man in his evolution towards perfection. It seems to me that though my ideas are born out of the past, yet they reach me perfected. They come to me full-blown on the cosmic tide, all ancient errors smoothed away.'[3] In all this there was also an evident pedagogic vocation, as is demonstrated by the famous series of photographs in which,

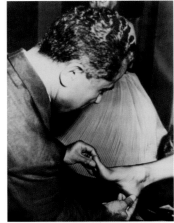

Salvatore Ferragamo touching the arch of the foot of one of his customers before taking its measurements, 1958. Ever since his childhood he had expressed a specific desire to care for the body of his customers by means of an understanding of the nature and needs of the foot

Ferragamo had a strong pedagogic vocation as is demonstrated by the series of photographs in which, as if in some workshop from the ancient past, the master explains the tricks of the trade to a young apprentice

as if in an ancient workshop from the past, the master explains the tricks of the trade to a young apprentice. Thus the dreams referred to in the title of the autobiography came to assume the guise of prophetic visions, in part arriving from remote dimensions and in other ways incubated by desire, according to the techniques of oneiromancy that had been illustrated by Artemidorus Daldianus in antiquity. His work for Hollywood, from D. W. Griffith's cowboy boots to the sandals for Cecil B. DeMille's *The Ten Commandments* (1923), is a demonstration of this. DeMille, moreover, had a specific interest in fashion, which appears as a theme in some risqué films he made on contemporary subjects. The titles, always linked to stories of betrayal and troubled love affairs, are the proverbial ones of *Old Wives for New* (1918) and *Why Change Your Wife?* (1920), in which the stunning costumes of exotic taste were designed by Natacha Rambova, best-known for her marriage to Rodolfo Valentino. The celebrated biblical colossal, released shortly after the discovery of the treasure in the tomb of Tutankhamon that had revived the craze for things Egyptian, allowed Ferragamo to bring back some of these ghosts from the past. In fact a number of things created by his imagination later turned out to have historical grounds: the shoes he designed for the pharaoh were found in an image in the Cairo Museum. In the same way his famous wedges proved to have a direct historical precedent in an archaeological find at the so-called Villa del Boccaccio, showing that his 'revolutionary' creation was 'at least six hundred years old.'[4] So the master of footwear stands precisely in the middle of the theosophical century, a period in which, against a background of accelerating industrial progress, people increasingly turned back to ancient perceptions of the elsewhere, rediscovering remote resonances of aesthetic activity. Anatomy was one of the main cores of this knowledge, at once new and old, that founds its own first principle in the relationship between body and space. It is no coincidence that Ferragamo studied this discipline with determination in his free time, at the university in America, in search of both scientific knowledge and wisdom. All these interests led him to develop a highly personal idea of the relationship between foot and body that was determined through the use of a plumb line, permitting him to make shoes that exactly fitted the forms of his customers' feet on the basis of an awareness of the modular nature of creation, reinvented over time in contact with different materials and designs.

And there was no other where in the world more congenial to spiritualist ideas than California after the First World War. These ideas were often proposed in a syncretistic form and it is no coincidence that Kahlil

Gibran's *The Prophet*, a collection of wise essays that was destined to exercise a vast influence, became an exceptional bestseller in 1923. In fact it was close to the place where the famous sign on the hill was to go up that the important Theosophical colony of Krotona, in which vaguely Oriental looks were the norm, had been founded in 1912. This was a centre with a huge library and its own publishing house, in which gymnastic activities were considerably important. It was later moved to the more secluded location of Ojai, in Ventura County, to make room for the studios of Hollywood. In Europe a similar extraordinary experiment had been carried out at Monte Verità in Ascona, a mystic-vegetarian community founded in 1900 and rediscovered in the Seventies by Harald Szeemann. Here clothes were made directly by members, which attracted many artists and intellectuals, including Friedrich Glauser, Erich Mühsam and Carl Gustav Jung.

So geometry and the spirit were the two terms of the discourse for Ferragamo, as presented in his account of a method of working that was also a vision of life. It is no accident that in his city of adoption, Florence, he found himself collaborating with various people who had similar aims in their research into aesthetics. One of the artists that he chose to illustrate his reform of footwear was Lucio Venna (whose real name was Giuseppe Landsmann). Over the course of his militancy in the Futurist movement, before going on to devote himself chiefly to poster design, he had signed with Emilio Notte *Il Manifesto del Fondamento Lineare Geometrico*, published in *L'Italia Futurista* in 1917,[5] which declared the aim of an anthropometric renewal of aesthetics, taking the human body as its yardstick. The other draughtsman chosen by the Florentine brand, Riccardo Magni, was also close to the colourful Futurist group called Pattuglia Azzurra. Yet in 1945 he produced for the magazine *Bellezza* two advertisements that were more Surrealist in style, presenting sandals against the backdrop of baroque buildings or a more 'orthopaedic' shoe set against an image of Milan Cathedral looming above the city in ruins. But the best-known portrait of the shoemaker of dreams, often used almost as a 'logo' of his business, remains the one by Pietro Annigoni, where a red scarf stands out against a sports jacket. The work, painted in 1949, launched the painter on the road to his international fame as a portraitist, after the experience of the 'anti-modern' group of the Modern Realist Painters.[6]

It is generally agreed that Florence has a long craft tradition, deeply rooted in the city's history and collective memory. Fashion first began to play a part in this process with the proverbial straw hats (echoing throughout the 19th and 20th centuries in the title of

Labiche and Michel's extravagant vaudeville farce *Un Chapeau de paille d'Italie*, or *The Italian Straw Hat*, later made into a film by René Clair and an opera by Nino Rota) that were long the main source of employment in various neighbouring towns. It suffices to think of Fiesole and above all Signa where there were many factories and where the museum devoted to this production is located.[7] Fashion, for centuries the monopoly of the guilds, dissolved by Peter Leopold's decree in 1770, became the focus of the activity of a cottage industry with a widely recognised excellence in the production of embroidery (spoken of at length in both *Sorelle Materassi* and *Le ragazze di San Frediano*), in which a superlative artist of the calibre of Emilia Bellini distinguished herself. Another widespread activity was, by ancient tradition, the one connected with tanneries and leather, whose memory is preserved in the names of various streets of the city. Among the many family ventures the Gucci brand began to establish a reputation in 1921, followed by the other names that have linked the place to a production of clothes and accessories that has slowly emerged into the limelight. A whole world therefore that presaged the first historic fashion show organized by Marchese Giovanni Battista Giorgini in the White Room of Palazzo Pitti in 1952, from which was born, after several previous attempts, the sensation of 'Made in Italy', closing the circle between contemporary invention and the art of the past in a mechanism that was to prove highly successful.[8] In this context Ferragamo's creations had an obvious importance, underlined by an ever growing international interest. The fashion magazines in America and Italy vied to be the first to cover the aesthetic and material inventions of the shoemaker of dreams. One of the models destined to cause a stir was the celebrated 'orthopaedic' wedge, which achieved success with the complicity of Countess Visconti di Modrone, revealing the extraordinary creativity of a designer who reacted

to the straitened circumstances of the time with a new style that was immediately copied everywhere. Many say that, especially in the striking polychrome model of 1938 that Natalia Aspesi rightly chose for the cover of her thorough work of research *Il lusso e l'autarchia* (1982), the principal reference was to the stars of the musical, who often did their singing and dancing (as in the case of Carmen Miranda, a regular customer of Ferragamo's) on what can only be described as platform shoes, but in this case it was a mainstream production. So the 'solid shoe' was the mark of the Ferragamo style before the war, while after it came a shift in orientation, with the *Invisible* sandal of incomparable streamlined elegance, created out of nylon in 1947, a design that helped him to earn the prestigious recognition of the Neiman Marcus Award. The model appeared, reproduced with mathematical precision, in the report published the day after the prize-giving ceremony by the *Dallas Morning News*. Another name given to this shoe that revealed at best the foot and that for this reason had lower sales than other models of the day, was *Eterea*. The imagery brought into play was that of an age of jet planes and fast-moving cities. These shoes would have gone well with Elsa Schiaparelli's sensational invention of the famous 'glass' cape, in reality made out of a plastic called Rodophane. Gianna Manzini, a well-known writer who recounted the world of Italian fashion under the penname of 'Vanessa' in *La Fiera Letteraria* and who often wrote about Ferragamo's inventions, summed up the impact of these materials well in an article entitled 'Tessili dell'avvenire. Sobrietà ed eleganza.' Pertinently citing Aldous Huxley and his dystopian *Brave New World*, she argued that some of the English writer's ideas were in reality rapidly coming true with the new productions. 'One more proof that fashion accelerates the time pace and throws itself without hesitation into

The famous wedges patented by Ferragamo in 1936 found a direct historical precedent in an archaeological find at the so-called Villa del Boccaccio. Here Salvatore Ferragamo and his wife Wanda are photographed with the historic creation, now on display in Palazzo Davanzati in Florence

'I have found,' wrote Salvatore Ferragamo, 'that the weight of the body falls vertically on the arch of the foot, as the plumb line shows.' This very personal idea is the basis of the system of measurement of the foot and the shoe that made Ferragamo famous all over the world. Ferragamo's studies of shoe size and width were the result of his attendance of anatomy courses at the University of California. In fact Ferragamo's first patents, which have been traced in America and date from between 1921 and 1924, were for medical applications and technical devices for injured limbs

Lucio Venna, a Futurist painter with a studio in Florence, made a series of advertising sketches (stencils on paper, 22 x 34 cm, Florence, Salvatore Ferragamo Museum) for Ferragamo in 1930 that reflect a sharing of ideas on the anthropometric renewal of aesthetics that took the human body as its yardstick

the mirages of the future, nourishing its eternal youth at the fountain of new ideas.'[9] The famous photograph of Ferragamo looking through the shoe sole made of vinyl, like a Bauhaus artist showing off a new object intended for industrial production, precisely reflects the atmosphere of the period following the end of the Second World War, when the 'airy' dimension, the quest for lightness, gripped all the creators of fashion after the disastrous years of conflict. It was the time when Christian Dior, who also received the Neiman Marcus Award in Dallas in 1947, achieved worldwide success with his New Look, which was at bottom an updated reinterpretation of 19th century models, in search of a revised romantic allure. *Corolla* was the name of the skirt that indicated a gauzy and graceful woman, one who would undoubtedly have been happy to wear the *Kimo*, launched by Ferragamo in 1951. This was essentially a Renaissance-style slipper inserted into a sandal and conceived as interchangeable, with different combinations to drive home the message he had always conveyed to his customers: for each garment a different and precise shoe, in accordance with the need for association with the clothing and the nuance of the moment. The materials used for creation, in times of hardship and of prosperity, reflect a continual, incessant investigation of the most varied substances, manipulated to give shape to the

shoemaker's dreams. Raffia (and its synthetic version: pontova), suede, leather, kid, cork, cotton, satin, antelope skin, lace, grosgrain, hummingbird feathers, hemp, cord, oilcloth and velvet were just some of the ingredients in a complex and varied work.

Florence, the place where Ferragamo ended up after a long journey through Italy in search of qualified staff who would be able to solve the problems he had encountered with the training of workers in the United States, met the needs of his spiritual quest as well. In fact the city was also a Theosophical centre of international standing and home to many prominent figures in the world of spiritualism who were known to him, and with whose theories he was already familiar. Arturo Reghini was a remarkable personality in the esoteric world: apart from certain contacts with the Italian right wing, the scholar's career had been pursued under the banner of Pythagoreanism, of which he was one of the greatest exegetes. A mathematician by training, he had expressed positions decidedly in favour of the revival of ancient faiths ever since the early years of *Leonardo* magazine, with continual references to the Roman world and paganism. One of his interlocutors was René Guénon, of whose *Le Roi du Monde* he produced a masterly translation. Moreover the French mystic was responsible for an important reassessment of the mythical figure of the craftsman, discussed at length in *Symbols of Sacred Science*. He traces the origin of its symbology back to the cult of Janus, who presided at once over the handicrafts and over the initiation into the mysteries, establishing a close link between two arts of transformation of matter. Someone else who was long in tune with the Pythagorean was Giovanni Papini, who became fascinated by it during the period in which he presented himself under the combative identity of Gian Falco, although he later distanced himself, speaking ironically about his mania for defining himself as the 'terrible brother.' Yet out of this exchange of intuitions came not a few of the Florentine writer's often splendid metaphysical fables, which greatly impressed Jorge Luis Borges, who considered the stories in *Tragico quotidiano* (1906) and *Il pilota cieco* (1913) to be of fundamental importance. The scholar's home territory was the paradoxical but lively one of the Biblioteca Teosofica in Piazza Donatello, which had been a meeting place for the most diverse and eccentric minds ever since its foundation in 1903. Reghini had been director of this structure from the outset, and had been able to count on substantial private funding. In the rooms of this now vanished centre of diffusion of traditional thought, forgotten by most, many commissions were given to local craftsmen by the devout Theosophists, who naturally disdained industrial production. In the

Riccardo Magni, advertising sketch in a Surrealist style published in a magazine in October 1946

Pietro Annigoni, *Ritratto di Salvatore Ferragamo (Portrait of Salvatore Ferragamo)* Oil on canvas, 51 x 59 cm Painted in 1949, the picture launched the artist on the road to his international fame as a portraitist

writings he contributed before a fierce rivalry with Julius Evola pushed him onto the side lines, Reghini also set out to highlight a specific spiritualist bent in Florentine Futurism. This was evident in the research of Rosa Rosà and especially in her interesting metaphysical novel *Una donna con tre anime* (1918), as well as in Mario Carli's remarkable *Le notti filtrate* (1918) and the early work of Bruno Corra, author of the extraordinary novel *Sam Dunn è morto* (1917) which chronicled a genuine outbreak of mediumship. In the city of the Lily there was a vast following of Krishnamurti, the spiritualist messiah discovered as a child by a collaborator of Annie Besant and theorist of a fusion of Eastern and Western elements that formed the basis of the organization known as the Order of the Star. He has been celebrated among others by Van Morrison in a famous album: *No Guru, No Method, No Teacher* (1986). Krishnamurti was often in Florence, where in the Thirties he was portrayed by Giovanni Costetti as an extremely elegant spellbinder, surrounded by an audience of enthusiastic female disciples. The portrait may refer to a famous conference held by Krishnamurti in 1937, and the guru of modern times came back to speak on the banks of the Arno again in 1953. The person who acted as a go-between with this figure was a Florentine woman devoted to yoga who came from a family of great prestige, long involved with the musical scene: Vanda Scaravelli. In Switzerland, a part of Europe that has

always been open to spiritualist experiences (as the composer Giacinto Scelsi has analysed in extraordinary fashion in his autobiography *Il sogno 101*), Vanda Scaravelli had taken lessons from B. K. S. Iyengar, one of the greatest teachers of yoga, and had gone on to develop her own method of meditation, summed up after years of research in her remarkable book *Awakening the Spine* (1991). Her husband Luigi Scaravelli, a very well-known philosopher in the Thirties, had also been the first to introduce the ideas of Martin Heidegger into Italy. So our prophet was quite at home in intellectual circles, as suggested by the sketch offered of him by Irene Brin: 'He became a tall, slender, olive-skinned young man, popular at the congresses: an excellent tennis player, it seems. A studio in Berlin offered him a contract for a propaganda film on the problems of the spirit and love.'[10] Costetti, as if joining up the dots of the picture of a world filled with resonances, has also left the passionate portrait of Lanza del Vasto.[11] The latter, long resident in Tuscany before moving to France, acted as an intermediary with contemporary India, popularizing a body of thought known only to a few in Europe at the time. His most famous book is *Le Pélerinage aux Sources* (1943, published in English as *Return to the Source*, 1971): his initiation to the world of the spirit came, as happened for many Westerners in the 20th century, through fashion. As Virginia Woolf analyses with great subtlety in her story *The New Dress* (1927), a change of attire can to all intents and purposes lead to a new intellectual makeup. This is how Lanza describes his turning-point: 'At Madurai I experienced my first liberation: I was freed from my trousers, jacket

and shirt. [...] My new clothing is a broad and long piece of cotton cloth, white, plain and hand-woven. You gird your loins with it, crossing over the ends on the left side, twisting one around the other so that they become entangled, and in this way your clothing is held fast without the aid of any belt. [...] This simple costume of ancient dignity disposes the wearer to pure thoughts.'[12] In different ways all these figures were also interested in a revaluation of handicrafts, and it was the architect of Indian independence who did this most effectively by turning an apparently banal act like the weaving of the traditional *dhoti*, chosen as his sole garment, into an eloquent revolutionary gesture of protest against the colonial power, which had imposed British fabrics on the country.

However, the craftsman, entrusted with the task of metamorphosis, projects a magical image that always proves double-edged. On the one hand he is the figure who handles the complicated relations of art with nature, but on the other he sometimes also presents the image of someone who is in search of perfection. So it is no accident that the term used in Greek for this multiple function was *demiourgos*, which indicates at one and the same time a creature who works for the masses and his work, just as his social function was embodied in the myth of the god Hephaestus, saviour of men from barbarism by means of his inventions.[13]

Although fashion is considered to work on the surface, it has in reality often resonated with dimensions of spiritual search, especially when it expresses the desire for a radical renewal of dress, whether this stems from a political design or from a wish for aesthetic and practical regeneration. Madeleine Vionnet was the greatest of the inventors of clothing at the beginning of the century. She must be given the credit for having liberated women from the coils of corsets and girdles, in search of a body that could breathe, that could find its own rhythm outside the constraints imposed on them by tradition. The most famous image of this reserved, gifted woman, who sought a resonance of body and soul to the point of obsession, is the one that shows her at work on her little wooden dummy, intent on draping fabrics, on looking for discordant, unexpected cuts, and yet ones that were always dictated by the harmony of the body. Oriental spirituality was one of her guides in this singular, adventurous quest for new forms for contemporary world, carried out in the solitude of her workshop, flanked by a few exceptional collaborators like Marcelle Chaumont-Chapsal.

And it was in her atelier that Thayaht portrayed her in his magnificent picture of 1923. The Florentine-Swiss artist was the master of oxymora, a sculptor in the perfection of metal of allegories of movement like *Il Tuffatore* and at

the same time the creator of a garment that has gone down in history: the *Tuta* or overalls, to which he gave a decidedly glamorous dimension. It was a very sophisticated response to a fashion that in the years following the First World War was largely the gaudy mark of distinction of the 'sharks' of whom Bontempelli and Gadda speak: profiteers enriched by the war who liked to show off their wealth. In contrast to their boorish style the brilliant Michahelles proposed an item of clothing that was extremely simple to make, and yet one that at the same time had a powerful impact, and proved a certain success on its appearance. And this was not under the aegis of the Futurists who are usually associated with this creation out of convenience: in fact, he did not meet Marinetti and did not join the movement until 1929, while his designs had in reality been brought into circulation a decade earlier, after private trials on the estates of villas around Florence, where a cosmopolitan public had shown an interest in his research. The same thing happened with the amateur performances for which he designed costumes at a very young age. The first paper-pattern of the *Tuta* was published, it seems with the complicity of the designer and novelist Yambo, a science-fiction enthusiast, as an insert in the newspaper *La Nazione* in June 1920. There followed four years of intense collaboration with Vionnet, who had

The *Kimo*, launched by Ferragamo in 1951, was essentially a Renaissance-style slipper inserted into a sandal and conceived as interchangeable, with different combinations to drive home the message he had always conveyed to his customers: for each garment a different and precise shoe. It was created on the occasion of the first show of Italian fashion in Florence in February 1951 with the gowns of Emilio Schuberth

immediately been struck by that invention and had asked him for exclusive manufacturing rights to his clothes. The resonance that brought the two of them into communication was an abstract representation, one that fitted well with the Deco harmonies demanded by the Parisian scene. And yet it can also be related to the Pythagorean line that in the following years was sometimes echoed in the remarkable graphic research carried out by László Moholy-Nagy for the fashion magazine *Die Neue Linie*, published in Berlin from 1929 to 1933. An enthusiast for Theosophical scenarios, Thayaht's readings ranged from Swedenborg to Tagore, passing through Maeterlinck, and in 1930 he created an extraordinary table for séances on which the positions for the hands were engraved, which is now in the Seeber Collection in Rome.[14] In his magnificent drawings published in the influential *Gazette du Bon Ton*, the artist drew on the theories of dynamic symmetry carried out by the mathematician Jay Hambidge, which he had studied at Harvard in 1921, inserting them into an

essentially Deco context. In one of the theoretical and practical texts that announced the birth of the new article of clothing, shoes are treated as well, in particular in the advice to *tutiste*, or wearers of the *Tuta*. 'Then the woman who has the courage to do away with high heels will truly be a pioneer in the world of health and art. If girls were to go without heels until around the age of twenty they would gain much in growth and in health and would have no need to resort to a pretence to radically increase their stature.'[15] Thus health and spirituality became two sides of the same coin for this eclectic creator, at home in every field of the arts. He returned from Paris, when the experience with the Maison Vionnet came to an abrupt end, to an Italy that was slowly breaking off its contacts with the rest of the world and in which his intervention in fashion returned to a more avant-garde dimension, still like a very important guest but often regarded with suspicion in the national system of production. In 1928 Thayaht created four beautiful models, *Sirtico*, *Spaido*, *Canotto* and *Nauta*, as part of the National Campaign for the Straw Hat, for which he also designed the poster. Over the following years he proposed imaginative solutions, especially for sportswear. His new models had fanciful names, such as *femorali* (loose-fitting leggings), *ancali* (coverings for the hips, some with a sporty cut), the *toraco* (a sleeveless, low-necked singlet, with no buttons and a straight cut) and the *asole* (a light summer cap, with an adjustable eyeshade); they were more dreams than actual garments, and largely intended for the world of sports and seaside holidays. All elements of a 'synthetic Futurist wardrobe' that he summarized, together with his brother Ruggero Alfredo (Ram), also an artist but one who had less influence, in the *Manifesto per la*

At the time Ferragamo arrived in Florence, the city was also a Theosophical centre of international standing and home to many prominent figures in the world of spiritualism, some of whose theories are echoed in his autobiography. One of the personalities with an international reputation was Jiddu Krishnamurti, the spiritualist messiah discovered by a collaborator of Annie Besant and theorist of a fusion of Eastern and Western elements. He was often in Florence in the Thirties, where he frequented the cultural salons of the city. On one of these occasions he was portrayed by Giovanni Costetti as an extremely elegant crowd-pleaser

Costetti left the portraits of Krishnamurti and Lanza del Vasto, the latter long resident in Tuscany before moving to France. He acted as an intermediary with contemporary India, popularising a body of thought known only to a few in Europe at the time (Reggio Emilia, Musei Civici; Pistoia, Private Collection)

Evident in these sketches, made between 1921 and 1924 by Thayaht, pseudonym of Ernesto Michahelles, for the French clothes designer Madeleine Vionnet, is the inclination of both, artist and couturière, to Classical and Oriental cultures, seen as spiritual guides in the search for new forms for the contemporary world that would liberate women's bodies from corsets and girdles and from excessive frills.
Sketches for dresses, fashion sketches for dresses by Madeleine Vionnet, 1921–24
Pencil and watercolour on paper, 20 x 26 cm
Lucca, Private Collection

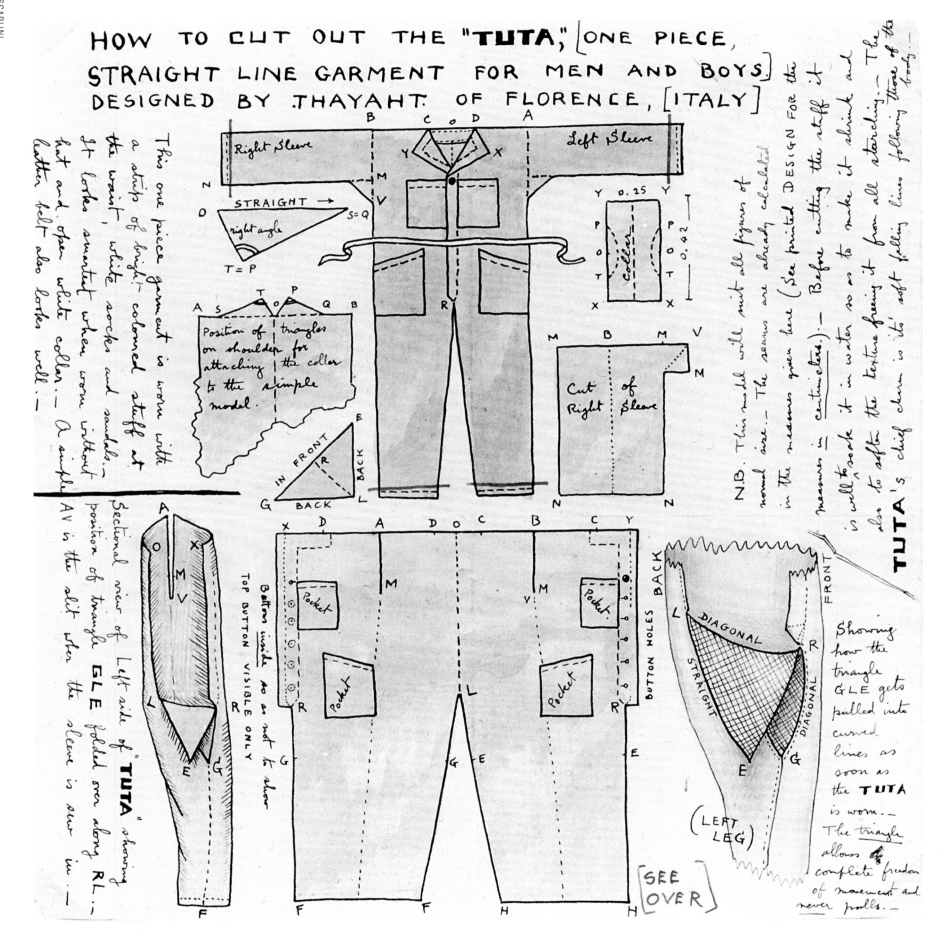

HOW TO CUT OUT THE "TUTA," [ONE PIECE, STRAIGHT LINE GARMENT FOR MEN AND BOYS.] DESIGNED BY THAYAHT. OF FLORENCE, [ITALY]

This one piece garment is worn with a strip of bright-colored stuff at the waist, white socks and sandals. It looks smartest when worn without hat and open white collar. — A simple AV is the slit when the sleeve is sewn in. —

Sectional view of Left side of "TUTA" showing position of triangle GLE folded on along RL. Button inside so as not to show — TOP BUTTON VISIBLE ONLY

Position of triangles on shoulder for attaching the coller to the simple model.

STRAIGHT → right angle T=P S=Q

Right Sleeve   Left Sleeve

Y 0.25 Y 0.42 coller

Cut of Right Sleeve

Pocket   Pocket   Pocket   Pocket   BUTTON HOLES BACK

(LEFT LEG)

DIAGONAL STRAIGHT DIAGONAL FRONT

N.B. This model will suit all figures of normal size. — The seams are already calculated in the measure given here (See printed DESIGN FOR the measure in centimeters.) — Before cutting the stuff it is well to soak it in water so as to make it shrink and also to soften the texture freeing it from all starching. — The TUTA's chief charm is its soft falling lines following those of the body. —

Showing how the triangle GLE gets pulled into curved lines as soon as the TUTA is worn. — The triangle allows of complete freedom of movement and never pulls. —

[SEE OVER]

trasformazione dell'abbigliamento maschile written in 1932, which starts with a categorical declaration: 'In particular everything that is bulky and constricting should be condemned. So we must eliminate collars, cuffs, belts, straps, braces, garters and all the symbols of slavery that hamper the regular circulation of the blood and the freedom of movement.'[16] Memorable are the inventions linked to his stays by the seaside in Versilia, where he drew attention to himself by driving around in a 'solar cart' fitted with a sail and worked with a young male model whom he used to create sophisticated body paintings, halfway between science-fiction and tribal decorations. In fact a world of rent boys appears in his works of the Thirties, with results not unlike certain contemporary pencil portraits by de Pisis. In 1950, many years after their last meeting, the artist re-established contact with Madeleine Vionnet, who in the meantime had gone through various reverses of fortune. Resuming a conversation interrupted for years, the great couturière returned to subjects dear to both of them and asked Thayaht, referring to the aforementioned book on India: 'Do you know Lanza del Vasto's *Le Pélerinage aux Sources*, published by Denoël, in Paris? It has been translated: it's more of a homage to Gandhi, to his doctrine [...] After reading it, when I picked up my pen to write to the publisher, I had the impression that it would help you to

express yourself, to find your way better'.[17] The old lady did not know that the mystical writer had in fact invited the artist to Berlin in 1930 to see an exhibition of spiritualist painters who presented their work collectively as the group Arco. Vionnet struck the same notes in a later letter, referring to her reading of Spalding's book *Life and Teaching of the Masters of the Far East*, in which 'many things leave her perplexed, but she is pleased to manage to grasp the essential'.[18] The Orient, a place where traditions were maintained and where the historic textile arts still existed, played an important role in the fashion of the 1900s. It all started with the inspiration for the Ballets Russes, which left a mark on the decade of Paul Poiret's runaway triumphs, before the First World War. Ferragamo also devoted part of his vast output to the theme, creating shoes literally from *A Thousand and One Nights* for one of his most faithful customers, Indira Devi, the Maharani of Cooch Behar (now in West Bengal), to whom he dedicated a bright red sandal adorned with precious embroidery. The classic mule was moreover a typical and much appreciated product of the house. In 1938 many models had begun to appear in the magazines: babouches, frequently with a very pointed toe, or a decidedly turned-up one, in a range of colours from gold to red, often with polychrome inserts. Elsa Schiaparelli, portrayed along with Ferragamo on the

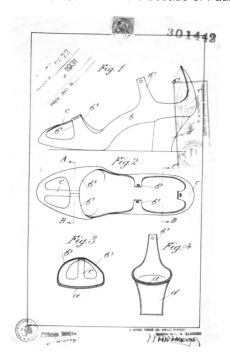

The Florentine-Swiss artist Thayaht was the creator of a garment that has gone down in history, the *Tuta* or overalls, to which he gave a glamorous dimension. The first paper-pattern was published as an insert in *La Nazione* in June 1920

Thayaht portrayed wearing the *Tuta* he invented. In 1928 the artist also designed straw hats as part of the national campaign for the relaunch of this production. He invented models of shoes too, such as the celebrated 'sandal with eyes' that appears in one of the photos and that has been the symbol of children's shoes in Italy for generations

An echo of the experiments with clothing and accessories carried out by Thayaht and the Futurists can be found in this 1931 patent for one of Ferragamo's inventions (no. 301442) regarding a means of producing a set of footwear from a single piece of leather. In the mid-Twenties Thayaht began to consider the Futurist influences that were returning to the country in innumerable forms through imported fashion, after having been appreciated and exploited by foreigners. He also referred to Ferragamo's models of shoes that had just arrived from America: 'The mix of leathers with different grains and colours, and the special profile that seems to increase the lightness of the step forward, which at once we find pleasing and is in effect elegant, that practical combination of tactile qualities (leather, canvas, rubber) is derived from Italian Futurism'

occasion of the historic ball held at Palazzo Strozzi in 1946 on the theme of *The Italian Woman over the Centuries*, in 1948 had embarked on her extraordinary work of innovation in fashion, recruiting an entire group of Armenian *tricoteuses*. These ladies created extremely traditional jumpers that, with Schiaparelli's (alias Schiap) touch, became modern and chic.[19] The allusions to that world were also declarations of interest in various forms of spirituality, a playing around with references to spiritualism that even led the fashion designer to give her white Tibetan dog the name Gourou Gourou.

Paco Rabanne remained in the history of fashion as the master of new materials, of which he declared himself a manipulator in unheard-of ways. This was evident right from his famous first show of 1964, at which a group of black models wore dresses made of sheet metal, Rhodoid and other new materials, dancing frenziedly to the *outré* music of Pierre Boulez's *Le marteau sans maître*. In this case too geometry and visions went hand in hand: the fashion designer has always admitted his interest in mediums, which on one occasion even caused him some image problems, when in 1999 his prediction that the Mir space capsule was going to fall on Paris was reported in the newspapers. The choice of an absolute geometry, which stemmed in part from his frequentation of leading figures in the French avant-garde of the period, also had its roots in his thorough studies of architecture and in images of other times, in the past and the future. Moreover, in 1991 the fashion designer had also proposed a personal vision of 'prophetic fashion,'[20] defining in a

simple series of associations a relationship between forms and periods, such as the establishment of a clear division between sex and brain by the very tight belt in times of puritanism. All in the certainty that 'the couturier is able to hear the music of the spheres,' tuning himself in effectively to the elsewhere. For this reason his alter-ego which appears in the wings of a fashion parade was given the appearance of a clairvoyant armed with pliers and wrench in the enchanting parody of the fashion world *Who Are You, Polly Magoo?* made by the fashion photographer William Klein (1966). In the opening sequence the beautiful model Donyale Luna is dressed in an outfit of sheet metal that no one could possibly wear. After Ferragamo shoes have often been reinterpreted in daring and unexpected forms: they immediately declare their own precise symbolic power of representation. Perhaps no one has summed up the possible resonances of footwear better than Filippo de Pisis, in a note written in 1921. 'Two poor white shoes, out of season, dirty, faded in the mud, can present a sight of pitiful sadness to a delicate eye [...] on the other hand a fine pair of polished and well-made shoes can be a delight.'[21] For his part the shoemaker of dreams had illustrated every possible significance of the concept of footwear, in the process revolutionizing fashion photography too, which for the first time began to devote massive attention to the subject with him. 'He leaves his name engraved on the 20th century in part for that memorable creation, the Rainbow multicoloured wedge sandal made for Judy Garland after the success of the *Wizard of Oz*'.[22]

The image of the *Rainbow* sandal with a multicoloured wedge created for Judy Garland after the success of the *Wizard of Oz* sums up Ferragamo's creativity, capable of revolutionizing not just the concept of footwear but also fashion photography, which for the first time began to devote massive attention to the subject with him

[1] S. Ferragamo, *Shoemaker of Dreams* (original edition London: George G. Harrap & Co. Ltd, 1957; Livorno: Sillabe, 2006), p. 162. For an analysis of Ferragamo's work see, among others: *Leaders of Fashion. Salvatore Ferragamo (1898–1960)*, exhibition catalogue (Florence, Palazzo Strozzi, May 4th – June 30th 1985), edited by K. Aschengreen Piacenti, S. Ricci, G. Vergani (Florence: Centro Di, 1985).
[2] Ivi, p. 26.
[3] Ivi, pp. 59–60.
[4] Ivi, p. 141.
[5] 'Il Manifesto del Fondamento Lineare Geometrico': the text can be found in what remains the principal critical assessment of Venna: M. Fidolini, *Lucio Venna. Il siero futurista* (Pontedera: Bandecchi e Vivaldi, 1988).
[6] For a history of the impact of this portrait see the entry on the picture in the catalogue of the exhibition *I Pittori Moderni della Realtà*, edited by M. Fagiolo Dell'Arco (Florence: Vallecchi, 1984), p. 29.
[7] On the subject of straw see R. Lunardi, 'La lavorazione della paglia,' in *Arti Fiorentine. La grande storia dell'Artigianato*, edited by R. Spinelli (Florence: Giunti, 2003), pp. 211–227.
[8] See S. Ricci, 'L'artigianato della moda', ivi, pp. 229–256.

[9] G. Manzini, 'Tessili dell'avvenire. Sobrietà e eleganza,' in *La moda di Vanessa* (Palermo: Sellerio, 2003), pp. 201–209, in particular p. 202.
[10] I. Brin, 'Krishnamurti', in *Usi e costumi 1920-1940* (Palermo: Sellerio, 1981), p. 138. For a close examination of the impact of the theosophist and a view of the role played by esoteric movements in the Italian culture of the early 20th century, see F. Ponzetta, *L'esoterismo nella cultura di destra. L'esoterismo nella cultura di sinistra* (Siena: Jubal, 2005).
[11] Reproductions of the picture can be found in *Giovanni Costetti*, edited by R. Barilli, F. Ambrosetti (Milan: Mazzotta, 1983), on pp. 80, 81 and 99 respectively.
[12] Lanza del Vasto, *Le Pélerinage aux Sources* (Paris: Denoël, 1943). English ed., *Return to the Source* (London: Rider, 1971). The passage has been translated from the Italian edition, *Pellegrinaggio alle sorgenti. Incontro con Gandhi e con l'India* (Milan: Il Saggiatore, 2005), pp. 23–24.
[13] For an analysis of the direct and metaphorical meanings of the craftsman, see the thorough research carried out by R. Sennett in *The Craftsman* (New Haven-London: Yale University Press, 2008), in particular pp. 21 ff.

[14] There is a picture of the table in Various Authors, *Thayaht. Futurista irregolare*, exhibition catalogue (Rovereto, MART, June 11th – September 11th 2005) edited by D. Fonti (Milan: Skira, 2005), p. 124.
[15] Thayaht, *Tuta femminile. Avvertimenti alle tutiste*, leaflet, ivi, p. 373.
[16] Thayaht-Ram, *Manifesto per la trasformazione dell'abbigliamento maschile*, typewritten manifesto, 1932, now ivi, pp. 404-407, in particular p. 405.
[17] M. Vionnet, *Lettera a Thayaht*, April 18th 1950, ivi, p. 358
[18] M. Vionnet, *Lettera a Thayaht*, May 1950, ivi, p. 364
[19] E. Schiaparelli, *Shocking Life* (London: Victoria and Albert Museum, 2007), pp. 43 ff.
[20] P. Rabanne, *Trajectoire. D'une vie à l'autre* (Paris: J'ai lu, 1991), p. 147. In this book he speaks at length of the relationship between fashion and vision.
[21] F. de Pisis, 'Le scarpe tristi,' in *Adamo o dell'eleganza. Per un'estetica del vestire*, edited by B. de Pisis, S. Zanotto (Milan: Abscondita, 2005), p. 45.
[22] G. Serafini, 'Un archetipo da inventare?,' in S. Mazza, *Scarperentola* (Milan: Idea Books, 1993), p. 17.

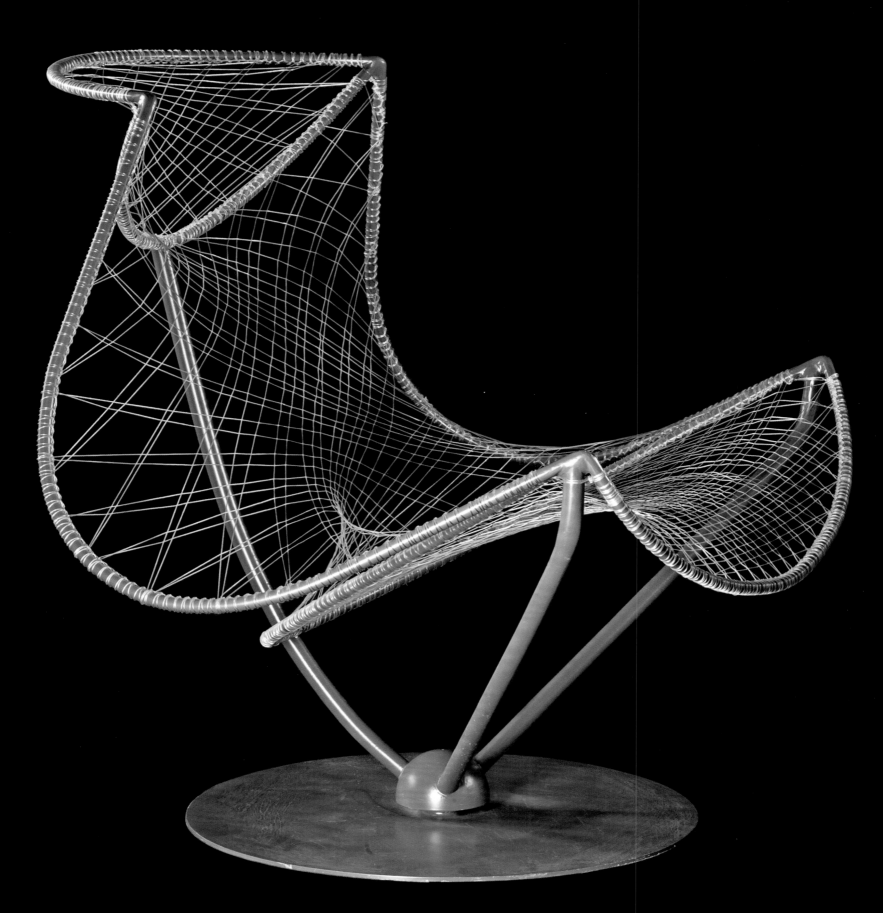

Conti, Forlani and Grassi, *Antiquariato 1962*, 1962, armchair in nylon mesh and wire for the 'Monofilo' Collection, Emilio Paoli. Florence, Marta Bindi Grassi Collection

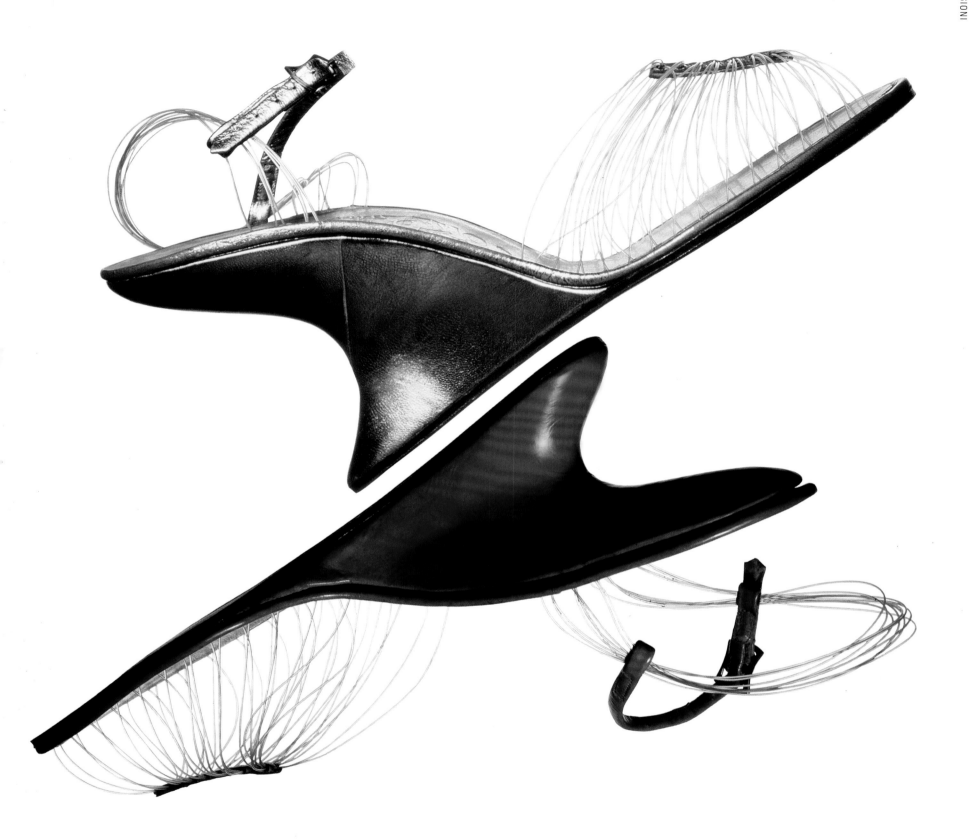

Salvatore Ferragamo, *Invisible*, 1947, sandal in calfskin and nylon thread. Florence, Salvatore Ferragamo Museum

'Making is Thinking' RICHARD SENNETT

THE CIRCULARITY OF IDEAS. PARALLELS BETWEEN THE CREATIONS OF SALVATORE FERRAGAMO AND RESEARCH IN DESIGN OF HIS OWN TIME AND TODAY

CRISTINA MOROZZI

Salvatore Ferragamo was a shoemaker, proud of being one and defined himself as such. Growing up in the workshop, he cultivated the craft and that connection between mind and hand which underlies many masterpieces of art. His devotion to working with his hands was similar to Benvenuto Cellini's for the trade from which his art was born. 'He was never ashamed of the foundry, its dirt, noise, and sweat,' writes Richard Sennett,[1] moreover, he hewed to the traditional craft value placed on truthfulness. In the *Autobiography* he recounts the struggle to extract gold, real gold and lots of it, from masses of raw ore—whereas even his richest patrons would have been content with the illusion of surface gilding. In carpenter's terms, Cellini hated veneers. He wanted 'honest gold' and held to this same standard of truthfulness in the other materials he worked with, even in cheap metals like brass. It had to be pure, so that things would look like what they are. Nor was Salvatore ever ashamed of his work as a cobbler. He had his picture taken wearing an apron and with his tools in his hands, in the midst of his wooden lasts reproducing the shape of famous feet. In this concern for the nature of the material emerges the attitude of a designer. Structure and material have always been at the root of Salvatore's creations. Each piece of footwear was a work that followed its own course of development, from statics to decoration. In each of them there was an invention, both stylistic and structural.

So to look for parallels between some of the models in his vast repertoire and design pieces of his time is not specious, although many orthodox theorists of design may think it is a step too far. Fashion and design scowl at one another, even though the borrowings are continual and obvious and there are numerous examples of creative people who have devoted themselves successfully to hybridization of them. Militant critics have always tried to keep the disciplines separate, emphasising the lasting character of design in contrast to the ephemeral nature of fashion, linked more to whim than to function, to the frivolous than to the useful. Paradoxically, even in our own day, characterized by synergy among disciplines, in Italy there is a reluctance to apply the word designer to those who devote themselves to the design of clothing and accessories. Chefs have become food designers and gardeners landscape designers, but in Italian, unlike in English, the creators of fashion are still called *stilisti* or 'stylists.' Fashion, dedicated to solutions meant for effect that distract from the social and innovative mission of design, is considered a dangerous temptress.

In the catalogue of the exhibition *The New Italian Design*, held at the Milan Triennale in 2007, I wrote: 'The crossing of disciplinary boundaries, cultural migrations and fusions of genre that can be seen in much of the work of the new generation of Dutch, British and French designers are not to be found in the new Italian design. The canny and advanced language used by young creators of fashion seems remote from the subdued and discreet one of young industrial designers. The new fashion designers create for a consumption rooted in the imagination that is meant to stir desire. The new industrial designers set out to provide responses to marginal everyday needs. In Italy, a country that has built an international reputation and economic success on "pure" design, fornicating with fashion, the sphere of the ephemeral, of luxury and of special effects, is regarded as unseemly. The new designers keep at a distance from it, almost as if they feared being corrupted, or at least to be misled. Perhaps, unconsciously, they are seeking a separation, shutting themselves up in a sort of soundproof chamber, cut off from the clamour of fashion, in which to play their delicate melody.'[2] Salvatore was an applied artist, like Gio Ponti was, who designed wonderful decorations for fabrics and china. And he was a designer, because he created in order to meet needs: those of the comfort and ergonomics of footwear. Functionality was the magnificent obsession that drove him to study anatomy in the US. He was besotted with feet: 'I love feet,' he wrote in his autobiography. 'They talk to me. As I take them in my hands I feel their strengths, their weakness, their vitality or their failings.'[3] But he also sought the special effect, drawing with a free hand on the whole range of colours and stock of possible materials. If it is the designer's mission to experiment, then Salvatore was a designer in the full sense of the word. He had the gift of an eye capable of seeing what could be done with any material. He knew, as Bruno Munari suggested in his essay *Da cosa nasce cosa* that 'things should be considered not just for what they are, but also for what they could be. In general one and the same thing can be examined from many aspects and, at times, the less obvious points of view turn out to be the most useful.'[4]

'There is no limit to the materials I have used in these fifty years of shoemaking,' he noted in his biography; 'I have used satins and silks, lace and needlework, glass and glass mirrors, feathers, the skins of ostrich, antelope, kangaroo, leopard, lizard, python, water snakes. I have used fish, felt, and transparent paper, snail shells and raffia, synthetic silk woven instead of raffia, raw silk, seaweeds and wool. [...] I have used beads, sequins, nylon [...]— do not be put off by its appearance of flimsiness—and transparent paper

"straw," which is string covered by transparent paper.'[5] Far from discouraging Salvatore, the disappearance of prime materials due to the sanctions imposed on Italy by the League of Nations in 1936 stimulated him, obliging him to experiment. In fact two of his most successful ideas came from just such improvisations: to be precise, from a box of chocolates and a piece of Sardinian cork. Attracted by the transparent paper in which the chocolates were wrapped he thought of using it to make uppers, stitching it together with coloured threads that shone through the paper.

His interest in poor materials was not, however, dictated solely by the need to find a substitute for precious ones that were becoming hard to obtain. It stemmed from the craftsman's desire to put his powers of invention to the test and from the intellectual curiosity stirred by his experience of the avant-garde of his time. On his return to Italy in 1927 he was undoubtedly influenced by the Futurist movement that proclaimed 'the use of hundred new materials.' In the *Manifesto della moda femminile futurista* published in 1924 the Futurists wrote: 'We fling open wide the doors of the fashion ateliers to paper, cardboard, glass, tinfoil, aluminium, ceramics, rubber, fish skin, packing cloth, oakum, hemp, gas, growing plants, and living animals.'[6] Salvatore flung open his doors to cork, cellulose, nylon, raffia... Nor was the experience of Elsa Schiaparelli irrelevant. Close to the Surrealists, a friend of Salvador Dalí and Jean Cocteau, Elsa transferred the Surrealist world metaphor into her clothes, utilising cellophane, rayon, Rodophane and other alternative materials with which Salvatore was also familiar.

The multidisciplinary approach of Salvatore the shoemaker has illustrious precedents in the history of 20th century creativity which demonstrate that there have been many similarities and frequent borrowings between fashion and design and that there is nothing unseemly about working on shoes, clothes and gloves, as worthy of being well designed as a coffeepot or an armchair. One example will serve for all, the Florentine Futurist Ernesto Michahelles, alias Thayaht. A painter, sculptor and interior designer, he was also a fashion designer and shoemaker. He invented the *Tuta* or overalls, published in 1920 in the Florentine newspaper *La Nazione* along with its paper pattern and the sandals with holes in them that he had made by a Florentine shoemaker in natural leather. Those sandals, which are still the uniform of Italian schoolchildren, attracted the attention of Madeleine Vionnet, who persuaded him to come to Paris to work with her. The many-sided artist Thayaht, unlike Futurists like Balla and Depero who also tried their hand at the design of clothing, played an active part in the birth of a modern Italian

fashion, involving himself, for example, in the national campaign of support for the straw hat in 1928, in the guise not just of fashion designer but also of organiser of the advertising materials. Then in 1929 he began to contribute, right from the first issue, to the periodical *L'Industria della moda*, the magazine of the Fascist National Federation of the Clothing Industry, making practical suggestions that were accompanied by clear and functional illustrations. He was an advocate of establishing a connection between artistic ideas and industry, experimenting with creations that combined aesthetics with practicality and reflected the new modernity in the radical simplification of their lines. His was not just a theoretical and ideal engagement like that of the Russian Constructivists. His overalls, in which he liked to have himself photographed, along with his unfailing sandals 'with eyes,' were much more wearable than Rodchenko's, to the point that they even caught on among the more intrepid ladies of high Florentine society, such as Marchesa Nannina Fossi Rucellai, who used to go to receptions in a coloured *Tuta*. In the magazine he gave commonsense and practical indications for the seasonal wardrobe illustrated with fashion plates, more as a specialist journalist than as an artist: 'Against the winds of March we propose a coat with a straight cut and black fur at the collar, white front and single patch pocket. The fabric can be a herringbone mix, or better a brightly coloured flannel.'[7] Thayaht did not think that working with fashion was inappropriate for an artist. In 1930 he wrote the *Manifesto per una Moda Solare*: 'Summer fashion is a sunny fashion; it is very likely that a Futurist fashion will develop out of this sunny fashion, i.e. a lively, colourful, simpler and more practical way of dressing than the current one [...]. What is needed is more colour, more uninhibited gaiety, more dynamism and less greyness, less rigidity, less prudent and starchy dignity, less pessimistic scepticism with regard to the problem of modern dress.'[8] Nor did he believe that designing fabrics and advertising posters was a secondary art. Indeed he put all his verve and acumen into fashion: exemplary, in this sense, are his 'signalling gloves' for the car, in two-tone leather, made by the Ugolini firm of Via Tornabuoni in Florence. 'With them,' wrote Thayaht, 'the rapid signal of the driver, given instinctively with the hand at the appropriate moment, is amplified and made more visible at a distance, so that it is clearly distinguishable even through the windows of an enclosed vehicle.'[9]
The fashion designer Paul Poiret was not only a couturier, but also a decorator and designer of furnishings and wallpaper who threw lavish parties in his luxurious Parisian townhouse in Rue d'Antin. Memorable was the one held in 1911 and called *The Thousand*

and Second Night, an apotheosis of Orientalism. Poiret did not feel himself suited to the design of products, but operated as a total artist to create a sort of total living: clothes and settings all in the same tone. He thought that clothing was the accent placed on the elegance that life ought to possess and squandered his entire fortune in pursuit of this megalomaniac vision. We do not know whether Salvatore Ferragamo had read Thayaht's articles. He certainly used colour, as the Florentine Futurist suggested, liberally. And he was never either starchy nor prudent. With the support of these distinguished precedents, we can now venture into a comparison between models of footwear and iconic pieces of modern design, discovering perhaps unconscious analogies that reflect an intellectual aptitude on Salvatore's part which made him open ahead of his time to hybridisations and reveal his readiness to take contemporary experiences in the various arts on board in order to attain new and unexpected goals in his own.
One of the most striking parallels is the one between the *Invisible* sandals with which he won the Neiman Marcus Award in 1947 and the chair made of nylon thread and wire belonging to the 'Monofilo' series designed by Conti, Forlani and Grassi in 1954, which won the Compasso d'Oro (the Italian award for good design) in 1955 and was then brought into production by the Florentine company Paoli in 1962. Salvatore got the idea for his sandals from one of his workers who was a keen fisherman and who had caught a large fish in the Arno with a new type of nylon line. '"The fish can't see it," he explained. It was,' comments Salvatore, 'the material I needed to complete an ispiration.'[10] Like the *Invisible* sandals which have an upper woven out of slender threads of nylon, the *Monofilo* chair has a supporting structure made of interlaced nylon thread. Luciano Grassi, who had a studio in the Santo Spirito quarter of Florence, liked to work with craftsmen and as a craftsman himself carried out 'home' experiments on statics and lightness, by blowing soap bubbles. The great variety of possible forms and the geometries that are created by their combination offered the possibility of carrying out formal and theoretical research directly connected with the study of structures and pieces of furniture. The idea for the *Monofilo* came out of the desire to create elements that could be used in any kind of environment, both outdoors and indoors, and that would have bearing surfaces of an anatomical shape, soft and elastic, transparent and resistant, light and airy, supported by a metal structure of extreme lightness, both physically and conceptually. From the behaviour of the film of soap stretched over closed three-dimensional perimeters were taken the fundamental notions for

Salvatore Ferragamo, *Sandal*, 1947, kid and vinyl, wedge heel made of wood covered with kid
Florence, Salvatore Ferragamo Museum

Verner Panton, *Chair*, 1969, Mobel Italia

Verner Panton, *Wire Cone Chair*, 1960, K2 model, Plus Linje

Salvatore Ferragamo, *Calipso*, 1956, sandal in satin with cage heel made of brass
Florence, Salvatore Ferragamo Museum

Salvatore Ferragamo, *Court shoe*, 1959, suede and leather with shell-shaped sole
Florence, Salvatore Ferragamo Museum

Arne Jacobsen, *Egg Chair*, 1958, model no. 3316, Fritz Hansen

Salvatore Ferragamo, *Sandal*,
1940, raffia and cork upper
Florence, Salvatore Ferragamo
Museum

Jasper Morrison, *Cork Family*,
2004, stools, natural cork, Vitra

Benedetta and Carlo Tamborini,
Gomitolo, 2008, cotton,
Diamantini & Domeniconi

Salvatore Ferragamo,
Sandal, 1937,
crocheted cotton and cork
Florence, Salvatore Ferragamo
Museum

Salvatore Ferragamo,
Sandal, 1955–59, satin
and Tavarnelle lace upper
Florence, Salvatore Ferragamo
Museum

Marcel Wanders, *Crocheted
chair*, 2006, resin, Droog

Studio Job, *Teapot*, 2007,
Bisazza

Salvatore Ferragamo,
Cork wedge heel, 1939,
**covered by silver mirrors
Florence, Salvatore Ferragamo
Museum**

the realization of the supporting surface; the 8/9/10 mm nylon thread, suitably woven and stretched over structures made of iron rod, was the practical outcome. The *Monofilo* was born out of the search for a new dimension of handicrafts that the *Mostra dell'Artigianato* in Florence had promoted around the middle of the Fifties. The inventive nature of the *Monofilo* was such as to immediately catch the interest of other professionals: Piero Porcinai, for example, used it in the beautiful setting he designed for the exhibition of the *Casa Abitata* held at Palazzo Strozzi in 1961. In 1954 the Milan Triennale put some prototypes of the *Monofilo* on display.

In one of those coincidences that are never really accidental, the architect Luciano Grassi, who studied in Florence as well as at the Hochschule für Gestaltung in Ulm, was passionately fond of design and active

as a designer of buildings, town-planner and restorer of old townhouses and also worked on the image of fashion houses, creating exhibition stands at Pitti Uomo (Florence) and trade fairs in Paris and New York. In the upper of the *Invisible* sandal, as in the *Monofilo* chair, the dense weave of nylon thread provides resistance and elasticity, creating an unprecedented look: one of nudity in the sandal and improbable lightness in the seat. In the sandal the nylon upper reveals and enhances the line of the foot; in the chair the nylon seat and back highlight the outline of the metal structure, giving the object the impression of a rapid sketch in ink.

Carrying on with the exercise of finding similarities, useful in showing that there exists an instinctive circularity of ideas in the creative sphere, fostered by the hunger of designers for research, by a propensity for taking chances that leads them to anticipate, almost in concert, future developments and by an eagerness for the new that places them on the same expressive level, even if they are geographically and culturally distant, it is worth pointing out the connection between a sandal and one of Verner Panton's chairs. Verner Panton, born in Copenhagen in 1926, wanted to be a painter but became a designer, translating his visions into futuristic forms that still look modern today. It is no accident that at the *Northern Light Fair* in Stockholm (February 8th – 14th 2011), Verpan, the Danish company that has brought back onto the market the majority of the light fittings designed by Verner Panton, presented new versions of his furniture and carpets, 'blessed' by the presence at the stand of Verner's wife Marianne Panton. The ever increasing success of the strategy of revivals is the proof that in the recent past there were formal values that have been able to withstand the ravages of time. And that innovative ideas are capable of winning people's approval even at a distance of years.

In 1955 Salvatore Ferragamo created a sandal with a cage heel made of steel. The steel heel was a product of his research into metal soles. The challenge was to provide comfort even with a rigid sole. He met it with a model of sandal that had a sole made of 18-carat gold, ordered by an Australian customer and created in collaboration with the goldsmiths of the Ponte Vecchio. Its decorative exuberance harks back to the works of Cellini, showing how Salvatore had always borne the ornamental lesson of the Italian cultural heritage in mind. In 1959 Verner Panton designed a conical chair made of zinc-plated steel wire, standing on a cross-shaped steel base, the *Wire Cone Chair*, whose form and interlacery recalls the cage heel of the 1956 sandal. It is unlikely that the Danish designer was aware of Salvatore's sandal, but the unexpected similarity demonstrates

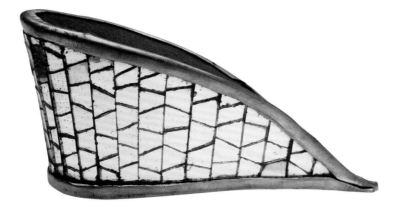

that the shoemaker Salvatore was, to some extent, a forerunner of the research into wire structures that has produced such evergreen masterpieces of design as Panton's aforementioned chair or the *Diamond Chair* of 1951, created by Harry Bertoia, a designer of Italian origin (he was born at San Lorenzo, Pordenone, in 1915) who joined his elder brother in Detroit, where he attended the Cass Technical High School, studying art, design and goldsmithery. Could it be that the *Diamond Chair* was partly the result of his familiarity with precious metals? The name itself suggests a probable connection. The *Diamond Chair* is certainly the product of an approach to design not unrelated to the methodology of artistic craftsmanship that was part of Salvatore's background too and whose most spectacular product was the sandal with a gold sole wrought by the goldsmiths on the Ponte Vecchio. The shell-shaped sole, Ferragamo's last important patent and employed in a series of successful models, has a precise parallel in the design of the time. The *Egg Chair*, a leather chair designed by Arne Jacobsen for Fritz Hansen in 1958 and still in production, with its wraparound shape, alludes to the form of that sole, which embraced the upper, restoring organic unity to the shoe. The extensive Ferragamo archives are a mine of material for study for all those who devote themselves to the design of footwear. Salvatore was an inventor. His formal and structural inventions, the product not just of talent but of study and a passion for experimentation, have a long life and go through 'courses and recourses,' as is demonstrated by the success of some revivals of his designs, more fashionable than ever. The analogies with design that can be discerned in the vintage pieces referred to above are even more surprising in some contemporary productions. Salvatore Ferragamo used to embroider the uppers of his shoes and Hella Jongerius, a well-known Dutch designer to whom the Museum Boijmans Van Beuningen in Rotterdam has devoted an ample solo exhibition (November 13th 2010 – February 13th 2011), embroiders vases. In Florence Salvatore proposed uppers made of straw and Patricia Urquiola, the exuberant designer of Spanish origin who has brought a feminine touch to the sector, has created for Driade the *Flo* chairs of woven straw. Salvatore covered heels with gilded mosaic and the

dazzling Dutch designer Marcel Wanders has covered large poufs with multicoloured mosaic. Salvatore made crocheted uppers and the young Danish designer Isabel Berglund presented a cupboard entirely of crochet work at the 2010 *Salone del Mobile* in Milan. Salvatore invented wedge heels of cork and the British designer Jasper Morrison, a leading exponent of the Minimalist current, has designed stools made of cork for Vitra. And the list of parallels could go on, growing more frequent today than in the past as a result of a return by the new generation of designers to working with their hands. Salvatore conceived and realized his own creations, convinced that the value of his inventions depended in part on virtuosity of execution and accuracy of workmanship. The new designers have gone back to the workshop too and are ready to get their hands dirty in order to construct daring forms, utilizing all sorts of material, from newsprint (Nacho Carbonell) to wheat flour (Forma Fantasma). What Richard Sennett defines as 'the calm industry' of the craftsman, which lay at the root of the production of some astonishing artefacts, was shared, as documented by his creations and the autobiographical confessions in *Shoemaker of Dreams*, by Salvatore Ferragamo, but it is also characteristic of the new generations of designers who have rediscovered the fascination of the applied arts.

[1] Richard Sennett, *The Craftsman* (Yale: Yale University Press, 2008), p. 73.
[2] C. Morozzi, 'Progetti omeopatici,' in *The new Italian Design – Il paesaggio mobile del nuovo design italiano*, exhibition catalogue (Milan, Triennale, January 20th – April 24th 2007), edited by S. Annicchiarico (Milan: Grafiche Milani, 2007), p. 6.
[3] S. Ferragamo, *Shoemaker of Dreams* (original edition London: George G. Harray & Co. Ltd, 1957; Livorno: Sillabe, 2006), p. 67.
[4] Bruno Munari, *Da cosa nasce cosa* (Bari: Laterza, 1981), p. 318.
[5] Salvatore Ferragamo, *op. cit.*, p. 227.
[6] Volt, 'Manifesto della moda femminile futurista,' from *Roma Futurista*, no. 72, February 29th 1920, in *Futurismo Moda Design*, exhibition catalogue (Gorizia, Musei Provinciali, Borgo Castello, December 19th 2009 – May 1st 2010), edited by C. Cerutti, R. Sgubin (Gorizia: Musei Provinciali, 2009), p. 236.
[7] Thayaht, 'Per la moda femminile,' in *L'Industria della Moda*, January 1929, p. 28, year XI, no. 1, pp. 28–29, in *Thayaht. Un artista alle origini del Made in Italy*, exhibition catalogue (Prato, Textile Museum, December 15th 2007 – April 14th 2008), edited by Prato Textile Museum (Prato: Museo del Tessuto Edizioni, 2007), pp. 136–137.
[8] Thayaht, 'Moda solare, Moda Futurista,' in *L'Industria della Moda*, June 3rd 1930, year XI, ivi, pp. 161–163.
[9] Thayaht, '"Cennatori": guanti bicolori per auto,' in *L'Industria della Moda*, August 1929, year XI, nos. 6-7, p. 25, ivi, p. 152.
[10] S. Ferragamo, *op. cit.*, p. 222.

'One can always tell from a woman's bonnet whether she has got a memory or not' OSCAR WILDE

INSPIRATION AND CREATIVITY FOR STEPHEN JONES

EDITED BY STEFANIA RICCI

English born Stephen Jones began his career as a hat maker in 1976 while was still a student at London's prestigious Saint Martin's School of Art. A visit to the Victoria and Albert Museum and the exhibition, *Fashion from 1900–1939* impressed him so much that he turned to fashion and millinery, following in the footsteps of a centuries-old English tradition. Four years later Jones opened a hat shop in Covent Garden and created his first collection. From that time he has collaborated with some of the leading names in the fashion world, including Fiorucci, Zandra Rhodes, Thierry Mugler, Jean Paul Gaultier, Claude Montana, Vivienne Westwood, Ungaro, Givenchy, Lanvin, Dior, Marc Jacobs, and John Galliano, with whom he has established an association lasting more than twenty years. Collaboration of this kind has made Jones a brilliant interpreter of other artists' creativity; at the same time he explores and expresses his own creativity, and this is unique in the fashion history. 'In language an accent never sits by itself; it adds intensity and much emphasis to a letter,' says Jones, speaking of his work. 'For 30 years my work has been about accenting something or some-one else. Maybe mine was never assertive enough to build my own language of fashion. I've always preferred collaborating with others to create the final fashion effect.'[1]

Despite this statement, the press, fashion scholars, experts and designers, and the most eccentric and demanding clients, have recognised Jones' extraordinary creative talent, from the time of his debut as a young student. His work after over thirty years is considered to belong more to the world of art than fashion in the normal sense and today it is worthy of being shown in the most prestigious museums of the world.

In 2010 in Antwerp's MoMu museum, Stephen Jones had a first retrospective on his work, with more than one-hundred hats on show. This led to collaboration with Ferragamo and participation in a new initiative by the Salvatore Ferragamo Museum in Florence on the subject of inspiration.

There are many similarities between Stephen Jones and Salvatore Ferragamo—as occurs often be-tween artists—notwithstanding their different formative years, cultural background, and span of time separating their activities. It is difficult to explain how this can be; it simply is. The artisan quality of Ferragamo's work can be seen in Jones' creations, even though the techniques are different, as is the piece's final use. The two have other points in common: a passion for their work, an obsession with quality, endless experimentation with material—from the most banal to the most unusual—and

formal rigour combined with a good dose of humour, as it is often the case that in the fashion world people take themselves far too seriously. Ferragamo put a rhinoceros horn on women's shoes in the Thirties and cork from bottles of good Tuscan wine on footwear for his most elegant clients, but he didn't mimetize them. Fifty years later and with the same nonchalance, Jones is putting a lion's paw or a painter's palette smudged with colour on the heads of women.

After Antwerp, collaboration between Jones and Ferragamo took shape in Paris and in Florence, where Jones visited the Salvatore Ferragamo Museum and saw Salvatore's shoes up close, although as a fashion history expert he already knew about their nature and value. Inspired by the Ferragamo models he saw in the flesh, Jones chose thirty hats from his archive which will be shown for the first time in Florence; the selection was made based on themes representing concepts to reading Ferragamo's style and work: colour, architectural shape, creative imagination,

material, glamour connected with Ferragamo clients who wore the shoes, the most beautiful actresses in the world, and Futurism, which is synonymous with inspiration from the world of art.

Jones decided to generously create three new hats, which will form part of the Salvatore Ferragamo Museum collection. They are inspired by the most wonderful models Ferragamo created in his professional career: the multicoloured wedge sandal invented for Judy Garland in 1938; the F-wedge shoe with kid and vinyl upper from 1947, which was on the catwalks in Dallas along with Christian Dior's New Look wear, a symbol of a fresh will to live following the horrors of the war, and the cage heel sandal, one of the most innovative patents of Ferragamo's ingenuity.

Jones' participation in this exhibition with his creations is an opportunity to find answers to those questions which have obsessed all who have worked on the project for this exhibition and seen it to develop.

Stephen Jones, *Tiddly*, detail of the invitation card for the 'Millinery Computer' Collection, Autumn-Winter 1998–99

Stephen Jones, *Triple Vision*, preparatory drawing, 'XYZ' Collection, Autumn-Winter 2010–11

Stephen Jones, *Sketches for the 'Covent Garden' Collection*, Autumn-Winter 2008–09

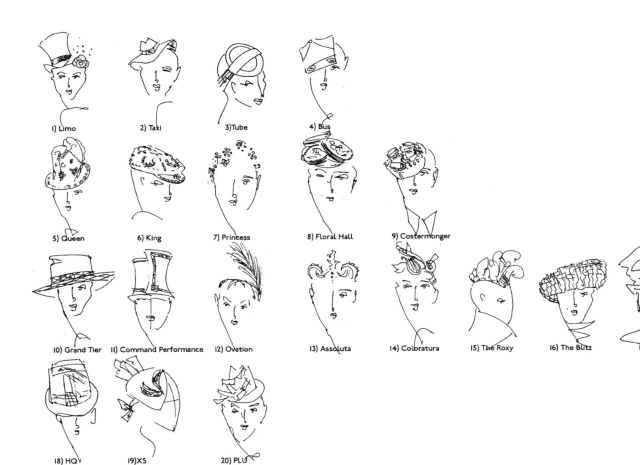

Stunning   Cognac Sauce   Untamed   With Love   Sumptuous   Tantrum   Expresso   Duchesa

Excitement   Diva   Hauteur   Cherry Flip   Drama   Satine

Coquette   Pericolo   Ego   Alta Moda   Blase   Crazy   Gala

STEFANIA RICCI What is creativity Mr Jones? How can it be defined?
STEPHEN JONES It's a form of expression which can be linked with the making of something. I don't think it can be explained with words. It's defined by the finished object.

SR When did you discover you had talent and a creative mind?
SJ I never did, I just carried on as naturally as possible (but from when I was five years old I was always best at Art at my class at school).

SR How much does technical know-how impact have on your work?
SJ In artisanal work, craft, art and talent cannot exist without each other. But at the same time you mustn't be hindered by your knowledge or lack of it.

SR Is one born or does one become creative?
SJ I think both; in any case the surrounding environment is very important. Encouragement of a passion, or vice versa its frustration, by friends and family are decisive factors.

SR Is there a recipe for young people looking to follow a certain path?
SJ Yes and I have to say the best recipe is British with our unique education system. In England you can do a Foundation course which allows you to find out the different pathways of design.

SR It's clear from analysing your collections that behind every hat there is an enormous amount of research which includes creating the shape and style and choosing the right material. In many interviews you've participated in, you don't hide the fact that you give special attention to research and pursuing countless subjects which inspire you, including history, art and movies, and this is demonstrated by your well-stocked library. Sometimes the themes are easily identifiable; other times they follow a non-linear trajectory and become mixed. In this exhibition we've tried to reconstruct, backwards in time, some of Salvatore Ferragamo's most powerful inspirational themes and we've done this with a certain degree of arbitrariness, as it is inevitable since some sources of inspiration are not documented and can only be deduced from the final result.

Stephen Jones, *Sketches for the 'La Prima Donna' Collection*, Autumn-Winter 2005–06

Stephen Jones, *Creation*, drawing for a hat

As we have a true creative mind on hand, we don't want to miss the opportunity to clear up some doubts.

What does inspiration mean to you, when do you feel it and how do you identify that it is the right inspiration? What is the path your mind takes from the initial idea to the final result which can be seen in the final product?

SJ Inspiration for me means taking the world and putting it into a hat. It's really based on a whim and you just have a feeling that the particular set of inspiration somehow is right. But that's your sixth sense, your intuition.

There is a certain logical path which is first-hand research, e.g. visiting a place, studying a theory or a subject through books, photos, travels. Then the sketching and then three toile fittings and technical fittings and then we do a dressing up where we try all the hats on together. Then I allocate the fabrics and three more fittings in the real fabric, etc. The process from initial idea to final product is very long.

SR We can't conclude this interview without asking a question on Salvatore Ferragamo. The curators of this exhibition felt it was natural to associate Salvatore Ferragamo with Stephen Jones and imagine shoes created by Salvatore worn together with hats by Jones. As such there's no harm asking how this experience was for you. What impressed you most about Ferragamo's work? What impressed you most about his personality and what aspect of the Italian shoemaker's creativity did you find the most amusing?

SJ Of course I never met Salvatore, but I've read about him in books, that he was a visionary and a creator of great character. Through this exhibition I've had the chance to get to know his work deeply. What I like the most is his 'jeu d'esprit,' his sense of play and his passion. I saw that like me he put his experience of life and work in a shoe.

[1] *Stephen Jones & The Accent of Fashion,* exhibition catalogue (Antwerp, MoMu, Fashion Museum, September 8th 2010 – February 13th 2011), edited by G. Bruloot, K. Debo in collaboration with S. Jones (Tielt, Belgium: Lannoo Publishers, 2010), p. 13.

Stephen Jones, *Design for the 'Musical' Collection*, Autumn-Winter 1992–93

Stephen Jones, *Technicolor*, preparatory drawing, May 2011. Hat inspired by the multicoloured wedge shoes created by Salvatore Ferragamo for Judy Garland in 1938

Stephen Jones, *Tap dance*, preparatory drawing, May 2011. Hat inspired by Salvatore Ferragamo's cage heel sandal from 1956

Stephen Jones, *Ingot*, preparatory drawing, May 2011. Hat in folded silk with layers of nylon tulle inspired by Salvatore Ferragamo's shoe with wedge heel and kid and vinyl upper from 1947

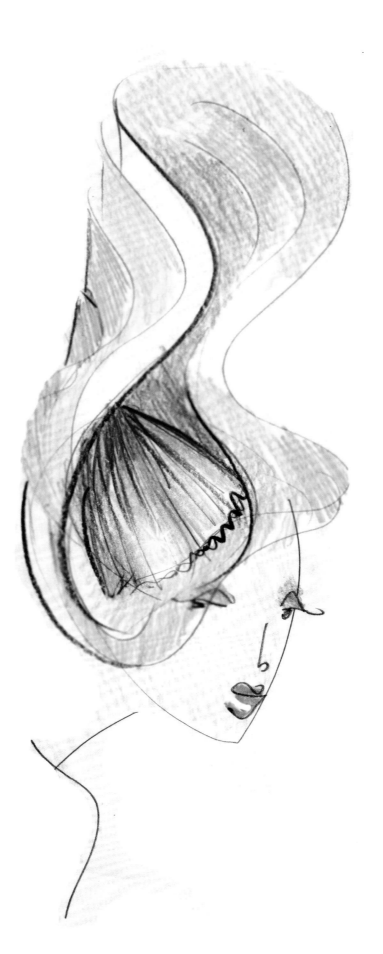

Stephen Jones, AWOL, 'Blah, Blah, Blah' Collection, Autumn-Winter 2000, tulle silhouette top hat. London, Stephen Jones Millinery

Stephen Jones, *Coloratura*, 'Covent Garden' Collection, Autumn-Winter 2008, operatic felt headdress. London, Stephen Jones Millinery

Stephen Jones, *Je ne sais quoi*, 'ABC' Collection, Spring-Summer 2010, straw and satin bicorne. London, Stephen Jones Millinery

Salvatore Ferragamo, *Ninfea*, 1937, antelope sandal. Florence, Salvatore Ferragamo Museum

Stephen Jones, *Niche*, 'Hollywood Regency' Collection, Spring-Summer 2004, hand painted satin architectural cloche. London, Stephen Jones Millinery

shape

Stephen Jones, *Gruau*, 'Blah Blah Blah' Collection, Autumn-Winter 2000, bidimensional wool crêpe cloche. London, Stephen Jones Millinery

Stephen Jones, *Colorama*, 'In Orbit' Collection, Autumn-Winter 1990, felt roll cloche. London, Stephen Jones Millinery

Stephen Jones, *SaamiAbbaGarbo*, 'North' Collection, Autumn-Winter 2002, Hindi embroidered sequin and tulle cap. London, Stephen Jones Millinery

Stephen Jones, *Multi-coloured Butterfly of love,* 'Souvenirs' Collection, Spring-Summer 1993, tulle biba hat. London, Stephen Jones Millinery

Salvatore Ferragamo, *Closed shoe*, 1942, upper in patchwork suede. Florence, Salvatore Ferragamo Museum

colour

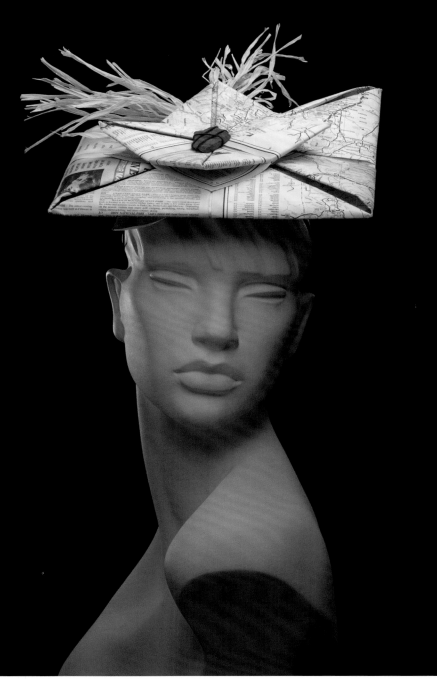

Stephen Jones, *Folded Paper*, 'Vanda' Collection, Spring-Summer 2009, origami paper flowers. London, Stephen Jones Millinery

Stephen Jones, *Barneys*, 'Xanadu' Collection, Autumn-Winter 1993, felt and rhinestone cloche. London, Stephen Jones Millinery

Stephen Jones, *À la carte*, 'ABC' Collection, Spring-Summer 2010, satin and organza fascinator. London, Stephen Jones Millinery

Salvatore Ferragamo, *Invisible*, 1947, sandal in calf, vamp with nylon fishing threads. Florence, Salvatore Ferragamo Museum

Stephen Jones, *Damn That Feels Good*, 'Celebration!' Collection, Autumn-Winter 1999, wood turban, London, Stephen Jones Millinery

material

fantasy

Stephen Jones, *Chic*, 'ABC' Collection, Spring-Summer 2010, bugle bead beret. London, Stephen Jones Millinery

Stephen Jones, *Witching Hour*, 'Celebration!' Collection, Autumn-Winter 1999, jacquard clock hat. London, Stephen Jones Millinery

Stephen Jones, *Serengeti 1935*, 'Murder by Millinery' Collection, Autumn-Winter 1997, stencilled felt paw hat. London, Stephen Jones Millinery

Stephen Jones, *Ecstasy*, 'Artifice' Collection, Spring-Summer 2007, photographic print of a mask. London, Stephen Jones Millinery

Salvatore Ferragamo, *Sandal*, 1940, satin and kid with platform insole. Florence, Salvatore Ferragamo Museum

Stephen Jones, *Tourist Trap*, 'South' Collection, Spring-Summer 2003, multimedia sun hat. London, Stephen Jones Millinery

Stephen Jones, *Vibe*, 'E = mc²' Collection, Spring-Summer 1998, cane window hat. London, Stephen Jones Millinery

Salvatore Ferragamo, *Sandal*, 1935, kid upper. Florence, Salvatore Ferragamo Museum

Stephen Jones, *Tiki Lounge*, 'Nursery' Collection, Spring-Summer 2000, Breton model in printed horsehair. London, Stephen Jones Millinery

Stephen Jones, *Cork Street*, 'Millinery Computer' Collection, Autumn-Winter 1998, nylon flocked toque. London, Stephen Jones Millinery

Stephen Jones, *Loopy*, 'Albertopolis' Collection, Autumn-Winter 2009, velvet and nylon fibre toque. London, Stephen Jones Millinery

Stephen Jones, *Roxette*, 'North' Collection, Autumn-Winter 2002, acetate ribbon headdress. London, Stephen Jones Millinery

futurism

glamour

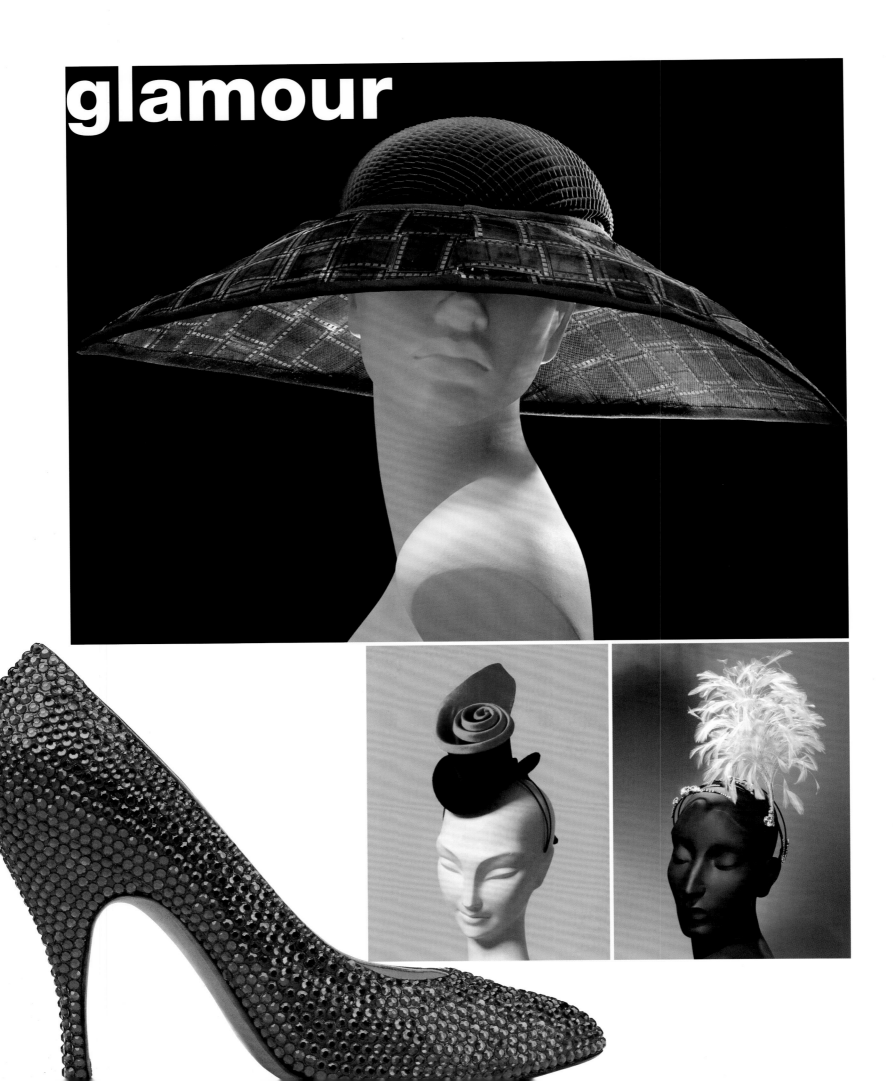

Stephen Jones, *Prequel*, 'Blah, Blah, Blah' Collection, Autumn–Winter 2000, film strip and pleated silk cloche. London, Stephen Jones Millinery

Salvatore Ferragamo, *Court shoe*, 1959–60, upper covered with rhinestones. This model was made for Marilyn Monroe *Let's make love*. Florence, Salvatore Ferragamo Museum

Stephen Jones, *Rose Royce*, 'Contours' Collection, Autumn–Winter 1996, velvet and satin top hat. London, Stephen Jones Millinery

Stephen Jones *Ovation*, 'Covent Garden' Collection, Autumn–Winter 2008, feather and jewel aigrette. London, Stephen Jones Millinery

Stephen Jones, *Santa Banana*, 'Tales of the Alhambra' Collection, Autumn–Winter 1984, jewelled plastic boater. London, Stephen Jones Millinery

THE FUTURE OF MEMORY

When Salvatore Ferragamo died in 1960, it was not just a thriving company that he left to his family, to his wife Wanda and his children, but also an archive of more than 14,000 models of women's shoes, dating from the Twenties onward and representing over forty years of activity. These constituted and still constitute the fundamentals of the brand's creative values and provide endless sources of inspiration for the designers who have worked for it over the years. Not just, in fact, those operating in the sector of women's footwear, but also people responsible for the creation of new products in the field of men's and women's ready-to-wear and accessories in both leather and silk have drawn on the abundant archive of patents and shoes built up over time by Salvatore Ferragamo, who had hung on to the prototypes of his inventions or bought back the more significant ones from his own customers. Thanks to the guidance of the Ferragamo family, the company has kept the DNA of the brand alive. Ferragamo's shoes are a testimony to this legacy and to the aptitude for research that, just as for Salvatore, continues to draw on contemporary events and developments in art, as well as on the craft tradition of the past. If on one hand, it relies on the inspiration or even the direct collaboration of contemporary artists for the creation of new products, on the other great attention is paid to everything that can document the applied arts of the past, through the acquisition of vintage products, books, samples and accessories that, once utilized, are added to the Collection of the Salvatore Ferragamo Museum and its library.
Stefania Ricci

Ferragamo silk ties,
Spring-Summer 1999

**Album of fabric designs
for man's waistcoats no. 13,
France (?), mid-19th century
Florence, Salvatore Ferragamo
Museum**

**Salvatore Ferragamo,
Prototype for a closed shoe,
1938, white suede upper
decorated with suede
Florence, Salvatore Ferragamo
Museum**

Album of textile designs no. 49, France, January-August 1897 / March-May 1898
Florence, Salvatore Ferragamo Museum

Prototype for a tie inspired by the *Iride* model

Salvatore Ferragamo, *Iride*, 1930–36, court shoe in golden kid and embroidered Tavarnelle needlepoint lace
Florence, Salvatore Ferragamo Museum

LIST OF EXHIBITION WORKS

The list of works follows the exhibition layout. Within each section, the artists' names are in alphabetical order and their works are mentioned in chronological order. The dimensions of each work are indicated in centimetres: first the width, then the height and depth last.

ROOM 1

1 Conti, Forlani, Grassi, *Antiquariato 1962*, 1962, nylon iron mesh armchair for the 'Monofilo' Collection, 105 x 77 x 80 cm, Emilio Paoli, Florence; Florence, Marta Bindi Grassi Collection. Shown for the first time at Palazzo Strozzi *Mostra dell'Antiquariato nella casa moderna (Exhibition of Antique trade in the Modern House)*.

2 Salvatore Ferragamo, *Sandal*, 1938, golden kid, cork heel and platform sole covered with multicoloured suede, 22 x 8.5 (heel height) cm. Florence, Salvatore Ferragamo Museum. The model was created for Judy Garland.

3 Salvatore Ferragamo, *Invisible*, 1947, sandal in nylon fishing thread and calf, wood wedge heel covered in red calf, 23 x 6 (heel height) cm. Florence, Salvatore Ferragamo Museum. Thanks to this model Salvatore Ferragamo won in 1947 in Dallas the Neiman Marcus Award, the Oscar of Fashion.

4 Salvatore Ferragamo, *Sandal*, 1947, golden kid and vinyl upper, wood wedge heel covered with kid, 22 x 9 (heel height) cm. Florence, Salvatore Ferragamo Museum.

5 Salvatore Ferragamo, *Calipso*, 1956, sandal in black satin, cage heel in brass, 22.5 x 8.5 (heel height) cm. Florence, Salvatore Ferragamo Museum.

6 Stephen Jones, *Technicolor*, preparatory drawing, May 2011, orchid headdress with straw, suede and multicoloured feathers. Florence, Salvatore Ferragamo Museum.

7 Stephen Jones, *Ingot*, preparatory drawing, May 2011, hat in pleated silk with layered nylon tulle. Florence, Salvatore Ferragamo Museum.

8 Stephen Jones, *Tap dance*, preparatory drawing, May 2011, gold cage top hat with black satin bow. Florence, Salvatore Ferragamo Museum.

ROOM 2

9 Salvatore Ferragamo, *Palazzo*, 1950, printed silk scarf, 90 x 90 cm. Florence, Salvatore Ferragamo Museum. Alvaro Monnini's drawing for Salvatore Ferragamo.

10 Alvaro Monnini, *XI Composizione (XI Composition)*, 1950, oil on canvas, 156 x 115 cm. Milan, Claudio Monnini Collection.

ROOM 3

11 Unknown author, *1° Una rivoluzione nell'abbigliamento. Il trionfo della Tuta. 2° Come si disegna la Tuta, Thayaht, il geniale pittore fiorentino, inventore della Tuta (1. A revolution in clothing. The triumph of the Tuta. 2. How to design the Tuta by Thayaht, the brilliant Florentine painter and inventor of the Tuta)*, around 1922, silent newsreel on 35 mm, B/W film stock, 16 frames for second, 12'. Florence, Marco Pagni Collection; Arezzo, Spe Distribution.

12 Unknown designer, *Parasol*, 1920–30, intarsia of Lenci cloth, diameter 64 cm. Gorizia, Musei Provinciali, inv. no. 3344.

13 Unknown designer, *Parasol*, 1920–30, intarsia of Lenci cloth, diameter 63 cm. Gorizia, Musei Provinciali, inv. no. 3687.

14 Giacomo Balla, *Linea di velocità più paesaggio (Speed line and landscape)*, 1916, mixed technique (pencil, tempera, sewing threads) on paper, 25 x 21.5 cm. Rome, Biagiotti Cigna Foundation, inv. no. BG/1.

15 Giacomo Balla, *Modello per cravatta (Model for tie)*, 1916, watercolour and pencil on shaped paper, 5 x 72 cm. Rome, Biagiotti Cigna Foundation, inv. no. BG/412.

16 Giacomo Balla, *Progetto di ventaglio (Design for a fan)*, 1918, watercolour and paint on paper, 51 x 39.5 cm. Rome, Biagiotti Cigna Foundation, Inv no. BG/ 5.

17 Giacomo Balla, *Abito futurista (Futurist suit)* around 1920, wool felt, 82 x 162 cm. Rome, Ottavio and Rosita Missoni Collection.

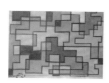

18 Giacomo Balla, *Motivo per stoffa con linee andamentali (Fabric pattern with moving and leading lines)*,1922, tempera and pencil on paper, 41 x 33 cm. Rome, Biagiotti Cigna Foundation, inv. no. BG/415.

19 Giacomo Balla, *Modello per stoffa, circolpiani (Fabric pattern, circle-lines)*,1922, tempera and pencil on paper, 40 x 32 cm. Rome, Biagiotti Cigna Foundation, inv. no. BG/414.

20 Giacomo Balla, *Motivo per stoffa (Fabric pattern)*, 1922, tempera and pencil on paper, 39 x 30 cm. Rome, Biagiotti Cigna Foundation, inv. no. BG/541.

21 Giacomo Balla, *Futur Panca (Futurist bench)*, 1925, painted wood, 69 x 78.3 x 25.3 cm. Prato, Farsettiarte Collection.

22 a,b,c Giacomo Balla, *Progetti per scarpe (Shoe designs)*, 1928–29. From top to bottom a. Pencil and Indian ink on paper, 20.5 x 13.3 cm, inv. no. BG/424; b. Pencil on paper, 14 x 10 cm, inv. no. BG/422; c. Pencil on paper, 14 x 10 cm, inv. no. BG/423. Rome, Biagiotti Cigna Foundation.

23 Giacomo Balla, *Studio di un'auto in corsa (Running car project)*, 1930, oil and enamel on wood panel, 44 x 30 cm. Florence, Private Collection.

24 Giacomo Balla, *Modello di golf (Model for pullover)*, 1930, tempera, pencil and ink on paper, 15.5 x 22 cm. Rome, Biagiotti Cigna Foundation, inv. no. BG/76.

25 Giacomo Balla, *Due studi di golf (Two pullover projects)*, 1930, pencil and tempera on paper, 31.5 x 21cm. Rome, Biagiotti Cigna Foundation, inv. no. BG/413.

26 Giacomo Balla, *Modello di gilet (Model for waistcoat)*, 1930, tempera, pencil and ink on paper, 15.5 x 22 cm. Rome, Biagiotti Cigna Foundation, inv. no. BG/80.

27 Sonia Delaunay, illustrations for the book *La prose du Transsibérien et de la petite Jehanne de France* by Blaise Cendrars (Paris: Editions des Hommes Nouveaux, 1913); stencils on paper, 45 x 65 cm. Florence, Biblioteca Nazionale Centrale, COLL.F.A. DELS. D.1.

28 Sonia Delaunay, *Variation sur forme géométriques, base triangle, bleu, blanc, rouge (Changing movement on triangular based geometrical designs coloured with blue, white and red)*, May 1924, printed crêpe tabby silk fabric, 37.5 x 49.5 cm. Lyon, Musée des Tissus, inv. no. MT 33721.

29 Sonia Delaunay, *Pois noir sur fond blanc, lignes bleus, cyan, rouges, jaune et vertes (Black dots on white back ground with cyan blue, red, yellow and green lines)*, July 1924, printed crêpe tabby silk fabric, 36.5 x 49 cm. Lyon, Musée des Tissus, inv. no. MT 33724.

30 Sonia Delaunay, *Décor de larges bandes ondulantes en noir, en rouge, rose pale, 2 tons de gris (Pattern of large undulated stripes in black, red, pale pink, 2 grey chromatic accents)*, August 1924, printed crêpe tabby silk fabric, 46 x 46 cm. Lyon, Musée des Tissus, inv. no. MT 33722.

31 Sonia Delaunay, *Décor composé de triangles formant une mosaïque (Pattern compounded by triangles making mosaic work)*, first quarter of the 20th century, printed crêpe tabby silk fabric, 45 x 23 cm. Lyon, Musée des Tissus, inv. no. MT 36923.2.

32 Sonia Delaunay, *Décor géométrique basé sur le jéu des rectangles en écru, rouge, gris, et noir (Geometrical pattern based on multicoloured rectangles: ecru, red, grey and black)*, first quarter of the 20th century, printed crêpe tabby silk fabric, 16.5 x 23 cm. Lyon, Musée des Tissus, inv. no. MT 36937.1.

33 Sonia Delaunay, *Décor composé de chevrons et de rayures (Pattern made by zigzag moulding and stripes)*, first quarter of the 20th century, printed cut velvet silk fabric, 50 x 17 cm. Lyon, Musée des Tissus, inv. no. MT 36969.2.

34 Sonia Delaunay, *Décor composé de zig-zag, de carrés (Pattern created by zigzag and squared designs)*, first quarter of the 20th century, printed crêpe tabby silk fabric, 49 x 20 cm. Lyon, Musée des Tissus, inv. no. MT 36970.

35 Sonia Delaunay, *Décor géométrique (Geometrical pattern)*, first quarter of the 20th century, cut velvet cotton fabric, 24.5 x 64.5 cm. Lyon, Musée des Tissus, inv. no. MT 37006.16.

36 Sonia Delaunay, *Rectangles imbriqués (Overlapping rectangles)*, first quarter of the 20th century, printed crêpe tabby silk fabric, 53.5 x 38.5 cm. Lyon, Musée des Tissus, inv. no. MT 33723.

37 Sonia Delaunay, *Décor géométrique (Geometrical pattern)*, first quarter of the 20th century, printed crêpe tabby silk fabric, 8.5 x 48 cm. Lyon, Musée des Tissus, inv. no. MT 37008.

38 Sonia Delaunay, *Semis de carrés et de rectangles traversés de créneaux (Half-squared and rectangle forms crossed by half lines)*, first quarter of the 20th century, printed tabby silk fabric, 18 x 26 cm. Lyon, Musée des Tissus, inv. no. MT 36964.2.

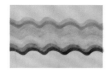

39 Sonia Delaunay, *Gros ruban composé de bandes ondulantes (Ribbon pattern created by waves)*, first quarter of the 20th century, printed muslin silk fabric, 70 x 50 cm. Lyon, Musée des Tissus, inv. no. MT 2168.8.

40 Sonia Delaunay, *Décor en bande composé de rectangles (Pattern with band made by rectangles)*, first quarter of the 20th century, printed cut velvet cotton fabric, 49 x 64 cm. Lyon, Musée des Tissus, inv. no. MT 36974.1.

41 Sonia Delaunay, *Décor géométrique (Geometrical pattern)*, first quarter of the 20th century, printed velvet tabby silk, 37.5 x 48 cm. Lyon, Musée des Tissus, inv. no. MT 33728.

42 Sonia Delaunay, *Composition sur la base du carré (Composition based on squared forms)*, first quarter of the 20th century, printed crêpe tabby silk fabric, 52.2 x 28.2 cm. Lyon, Musée des Tissus, inv. no. MT 36922.1.

43 Sonia Delaunay, *Sonia Delaunay: ses peintures, ses objects, ses tissus simultanés, ses modes* (Paris: Librairie des Arts Décoratifs, 1925), stencils on paper, 56 x 40 cm. Florence, Biblioteca Nazionale Centrale, F.A. DELS. D.2.

44 Sonia Delaunay, illustrations for *Juste présent* by Tristan Tzara (Paris: Fequet et Baudier, 1961), etching on paper, 30 x 42 cm. Florence, Biblioteca Nazionale Centrale, F.A.DELS.B1.

45 Fortunato Depero, *Gilet futurista (Futurist waistcoat)*, around 1930, felt, 47 x 63 cm. Rome, Renzo Arbore Collection.

46 Fortunato Depero, *Elasticità di gatti (Suppleness of Cats)*, 1936–39, oil on canvas, 108 x 84 cm. Prato, Farsettiarte Collection.

47 Marcel Duchamp, *Rotorelief*, 1936, print on cardboard, diameter 20 cm. Florence, Biblioteca Nazionale Centrale, COLL. F.A.DUCM.B.6.

48 Salvatore Ferragamo, *Labirinto (Labyrinth)*, 1927–30, court shoe with dark grey embroidered kid upper, 21.5 x 7.5 (heel height) cm. Florence, Salvatore Ferragamo Museum.

49 Salvatore Ferragamo, *Prototype for a court shoe*, 1927–30, velvet upper with decorations of glass flowers, 20 x 7 (heel height) cm. Florence, Salvatore Ferragamo Museum.

50 Salvatore Ferragamo, *Court shoe*, upper made with embroidered stripes, copy from patent no. 6937, November 27th 1929, 21 x 8 (heel height) cm. Florence, Salvatore Ferragamo Museum.

51 Salvatore Ferragamo, *Court shoe*, upper formed with zigzag stripes in different colour tones, copy from patent no. 6936, November 27th 1929, 21 x 8 (heel height) cm. Florence, Salvatore Ferragamo Museum.

52 Salvatore Ferragamo, *Two piece shoe*, suede upper with suede decorations, copy from patent no. 6959, November 27th 1929, 21 x 8 (heel height) cm. Florence, Salvatore Ferragamo Museum.

53 Salvatore Ferragamo, *Court shoe*, suede upper with suede decorations, copy from patent no. 6960, November 27th 1929, 21 x 8 (heel height) cm. Florence, Salvatore Ferragamo Museum.

54 Salvatore Ferragamo, *Sandal*, 1930, golden kid and black grosgrain fabric upper decorated with multicoloured grosgrain ribbons, 22 x 8 (heel height) cm. Florence, Salvatore Ferragamo Museum

55 Salvatore Ferragamo, *Prototype for a sandal*, 1930, golden kid and black grosgrain fabric upper decorated with multicoloured grosgrain ribbons, 22 cm. Florence, Salvatore Ferragamo Museum.

56 Salvatore Ferragamo, *Prototype for a sandal*, 1930, gold kid upper with painted circular decoration, bordered with chain silk stitching, 20 x 7.5 (heel height) cm. Florence, Salvatore Ferragamo Museum.

57 Salvatore Ferragamo, *Prototype for a court shoe*, 1930, black antelope with white painted circular decoration, bordered with red silk chain stitching, 21 x 7.5 (heel height) cm. Florence, Salvatore Ferragamo Museum.

58 Salvatore Ferragamo, *Prototype for a court shoe*, 1930, brown antelope with yellow painted circular decoration, bordered with green silk chain stitching, 23 x 7.5 (heel height) cm. Florence, Salvatore Ferragamo Museum.

59 Salvatore Ferragamo, *Prototype for a court shoe*, 1930, black antelope with red painted circular decoration, bordered with yellow silk chain stitching, 23 x 7 (heel height) cm. Florence, Salvatore Ferragamo Museum.

60 Salvatore Ferragamo, *Prototype for a court shoe*, 1930, golden kid upper with white painted circular decoration, bordered with black silk chain stitching, 23.5 x 9 (heel height) cm. Florence, Salvatore Ferragamo Museum.

61 Salvatore Ferragamo, *Iride*, 1930–36, court shoe in golden kid and embroidered Tavarnelle needlepoint lace, 22 x 8 (heel height) cm. Florence, Salvatore Ferragamo Museum.

62 Salvatore Ferragamo, *Prototype for a court shoe*, 1930–35, painted canvas, embroidered with chain silk stitching, 22,5 cm. Florence, Salvatore Ferragamo Museum.

63 Salvatore Ferragamo, *Prototype for a court shoe*, 1930–35, beige painted kid, embroidered with silk chain stitching, 22,5 cm. Florence, Salvatore Ferragamo Museum.

64 Salvatore Ferragamo, *Court shoe*, 1930–35, turquoise-dyed fish skin, 22 x 8 (heel height) cm. Florence, Salvatore Ferragamo Museum.

65 Salvatore Ferragamo, *Two piece shoe*, 1930–35, embroidered black satin with Tavarnelle needlepoint lace, 24 x 8 (heel height) cm. Florence, Salvatore Ferragamo Museum.

66 Salvatore Ferragamo, *Prototype for a court shoe*, 1930–35, upper in green calf and mechanised silk chain stitching decoration, 22 x 8 (heel height) cm. Florence, Salvatore Ferragamo Museum.

67 Salvatore Ferragamo, *Laced shoe*, suede embroidered upper with silk chain stitching, copy from patent no. 7867, February 21st 1931, 21 x 8 (heel height) cm. Florence, Salvatore Ferragamo Museum.

68 Salvatore Ferragamo, *Sandal*, 1935–38, blue suede and Tavarnelle needlepoint lace, 21.5 x 8.5 (heel height) cm. Florence, Salvatore Ferragamo Museum.

69 Salvatore Ferragamo, *Laced shoe*, 1935–38, multicoloured patchwork upper with embroidered cotton squares, heel covered with blue kid, 22.5 x 9 (heel height) cm. Florence, Salvatore Ferragamo Museum.

70 Salvatore Ferragamo, *Prototype for two piece shoe*, 1935–38, patchwork felt upper, heel covered with blue kid, 22 x 7 (heel height) cm. Florence, Salvatore Ferragamo Museum.

71 Salvatore Ferragamo, *Prototype for a mule*, 1935–40, printed multicoloured suede upper, 21.5 x 7 (heel height) cm. Florence, Salvatore Ferragamo Museum.

72 Salvatore Ferragamo, *Prototype for a sandal*, 1935–40, black satin and golden kid upper, 20 x 7 (heel height) cm. Florence, Salvatore Ferragamo Museum.

73 Salvatore Ferragamo, *Sandal*, 1936, kid and canvas upper decorated with patchwork embroidery, octagonal cork heel covered with blue kid, 23 x 4 (heel height) cm. Florence, Salvatore Ferragamo Museum.

74 Salvatore Ferragamo, *Prototype for a mule*, 1938, dark green felt decorated with cotton stripes, 22 x 7 (heel height) cm. Florence, Salvatore Ferragamo Museum.

75 Salvatore Ferragamo, *Prototype for a laced shoe*, 1938, black suede upper decorated with pink, yellow, green and pale blue suede, 23 x 7.5 (heel height) cm. Florence, Salvatore Ferragamo Museum.

76 Salvatore Ferragamo, *Prototype for a closed shoe*, 1938, white suede upper decorated with green, pink, pale blue and yellow suede, 22.5 x 7.5 (heel height) cm. Florence, Salvatore Ferragamo Museum.

77 Salvatore Ferragamo, *Prototype for a laced shoe*, 1938, red suede upper decorated with violet, yellow, green and pink suede, 21 x 7 (heel height) cm. Florence, Salvatore Ferragamo Museum.

78 Salvatore Ferragamo, *Prototype for a laced shoe*, 1938, black suede upper, 22.5 x 5 (heel height) cm. Florence, Salvatore Ferragamo Museum.

79 Salvatore Ferragamo, *Court shoe*, 1939, patchwork upper in purple calf and suede, 22 x 8.5 (heel height) cm. Florence, Salvatore Ferragamo Museum.

80 Salvatore Ferragamo, *Fiamma*, 1939, court shoe in black suede and brown calf, 22 x 8 (heel height) cm. Florence, Salvatore Ferragamo Museum.

81 Salvatore Ferragamo, *Sandal*, 1940, blue, green and yellow suede upper, 22 x 8 (heel height) cm. Florence, Salvatore Ferragamo Museum.

82 Salvatore Ferragamo, *Sandal*, 1943, red suede upper, platform sole and wedge heel in carved and painted wood, 21 x 7 (heel height) cm. Florence, Salvatore Ferragamo Museum.

83 Salvatore Ferragamo, *Sandal*, 1943, blue suede upper, platform sole and wedge heel in carved and painted wood, 22.5 x 7.5 (heel height) cm. Florence, Salvatore Ferragamo Museum.

84 Alberto Magnelli, *Explosion lirique n. 5. Les Baigneuses (Lyric explosion no. 5. The Bathers)*, 1918, oil on canvas, 120 x 120 cm. Florence, Private Collection.

85 Gino Severini, *Rythme de danse à l'opéra (Dancing rhythm at the opera)*, 1950, oil on canvas, 131 x 161.5 cm. Prato, Farsettiarte Collection.

86 Società Ceramica Richard-Ginori based on a design by Gio Ponti, *Nautica*, 1927, bowl in polychrome porcelain, 19.5 x 15.4 (maximum diameter) cm. Sesto Fiorentino (Florence), Museo Richard-Ginori della Manifattura di Doccia, inv. no. 5363.

87 Thayaht (Ernesto Michahelles), *Vort – motivo decorativo astratto ovale (Vort—oval abstract decorative motif)*, 1921, tempera and pencil on paper, 34.4 x 25.7 cm. Rome, Private Collection.

88 Thayaht (Ernesto Michahelles), *Sketch for dress*, fashion sketch for dress by Madeleine Vionnet, 1921–24, pencil and watercolour on paper, 20 x 26 cm. Lucca, Private Collection.

89 Thayaht (Ernesto Michahelles), *Sketch for dress*, fashion sketch for dress by Madeleine Vionnet, 1921–24, pencil and watercolour on paper, 20 x 26 cm. Lucca, Private Collection.

90 Thayaht (Ernesto Michahelles), *Sketch for dress*, fashion sketch for dress by Madeleine Vionnet, 1921–24, pencil and watercolour on paper, 20 x 26 cm. Lucca, Private Collection.

91 Thayaht (Ernesto Michahelles), *Sketch for dress*, fashion sketch for dress by Madeleine Vionnet, 1921–24, pencil and watercolour on paper, 20 x 26 cm. Lucca, Private Collection.

92 Thayaht (Ernesto Michahelles), *Sketch for dress*, fashion sketch for dress by Madeleine Vionnet, 1921–24, pencil and watercolour on paper, 20 x 26 cm. Lucca, Private Collection.

93 Thayaht (Ernesto Michahelles), *Sketch for dress*, fashion sketch for dress by Madeleine Vionnet, 1921–24, pencil and watercolour on paper, 20 x 26 cm. Lucca, Private Collection.

94 Thayaht (Ernesto Michahelles), *Sketch for dress*, fashion sketch for dress by Madeleine Vionnet, 1921–24, pencil and watercolour on paper, 20 x 26 cm. Lucca, Private Collection.

95 Thayaht (Ernesto Michahelles), *Sketch for dress*, fashion sketch for dress by Madeleine Vionnet, 1921–24, pencil and watercolour on paper, 20 x 26 cm. Lucca, Private Collection.

96 Thayaht (Ernesto Michahelles), *Sketch for dress*, fashion sketch for dress by Madeleine Vionnet, 1921–24, pencil and watercolour on paper, 20 x 26 cm. Lucca, Private Collection.

97 Thayaht (Ernesto Michahelles), *Sketch for dress*, fashion sketch for dress by Madeleine Vionnet, 1921–24, pencil and watercolour on paper, 20 x 26 cm. Lucca, Private Collection.

98 Thayaht (Ernesto Michahelles), *Sketch for dress*, fashion sketch for dress by Madeleine Vionnet, 1921–24, pencil and watercolour on paper, 20 x 26 cm. Lucca, Private Collection.

99 Thayaht (Ernesto Michahelles), *Sketch for dress*, fashion sketch for dress by Madeleine Vionnet, 1921–24, pencil and watercolour on paper, 20 x 26 cm. Lucca, Private Collection.

100 Thayaht (Ernesto Michahelles), *Sketch for dress*, fashion sketch for dress by Madeleine Vionnet, 1921–24, pencil and watercolour on paper, 20 x 26 cm. Lucca, Private Collection.

101 Thayaht (Ernesto Michahelles), *Sketch for dress*, fashion sketch for dress by Madeleine Vionnet, 1921–24, pencil and watercolour on paper, 20 x 26 cm. Lucca, Private Collection.

102 Thayaht (Ernesto Michahelles), *Sketch for dress*, fashion sketch for dress by Madeleine Vionnet, 1921–24, pencil and watercolour on paper, 20 x 26 cm. Lucca, Private Collection.

103 Thayaht (Ernesto Michahelles), *Sketch for dress*, fashion sketch for dress by Madeleine Vionnet, 1921–24, pencil and watercolour on paper, 20 x 26 cm. Lucca, Private Collection.

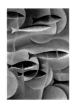

104 Thayaht (Ernesto Michahelles), *Pesci (Ritmi subacquei) (Fish—underwater rhythms)*, 1931, oil on wood, 50.3 x 75.4 cm. Rome, CLM Seeber Collection.

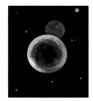

105 Thayaht (Ernesto Michahelles), *Paesaggio spaziale (Spatial landscape)*, 1932, pastel, coloured pencil on cardboard, 22 x 25 cm. Florence, Sandro Michahelles Collection.

106 Lucio Venna, *Advertising sketch for magazine*, 1928, stencil on paper, 22.5 x 32.5 cm. Florence, Salvatore Ferragamo Museum.

107 Lucio Venna, *Caligola*, 1930, advertising sketch for Salvatore Ferragamo, stencil on paper, 22 x 34 cm. Florence, Salvatore Ferragamo Museum.

108 Lucio Venna, *Coturno*, 1930, advertising sketch for Salvatore Ferragamo, stencil on cardboard, 20.3 x 30.5 cm. Florence, Salvatore Ferragamo Museum.

109 Lucio Venna, *Moderne*, 1930, advertising sketch for Salvatore Ferragamo, stencil on paper, 22 x 34 cm. Florence, Salvatore Ferragamo Museum.

110 Lucio Venna, *Nemi*, 1930, advertising sketch for Salvatore Ferragamo, stencil on paper, 22 x 34 cm. Florence, Salvatore Ferragamo Museum.

111 Lucio Venna, *Pompeiana*, 1930, advertising sketch for Salvatore Ferragamo, stencil on paper, 21.5 x 29 cm. Florence, Salvatore Ferragamo Museum.

112 Lucio Venna, *Sparta*, 1930, advertising sketch for Salvatore Ferragamo, stencil on paper, 22 x 34 cm. Florence, Salvatore Ferragamo Museum.

ROOM 4

113 Lucio Fontana, *Concetto spaziale (Spatial concept)*, 1964, oil, graffiti on canvas, gold, 65 x 82 cm. Florence, Tornabuoni Arte Collection.

114 Salvatore Ferragamo, *Sandal*, 1956, 18-carat gold upper, 24 x 9.5 (heel height) cm. Florence, Salvatore Ferragamo Museum.

115 Sano di Pietro, *Madonna con il Bambino (Madonna and Child)*, 15th century, tempera on wood, 32.7 x 40.5 cm. Prato, Farsettiarte Collection.

116 Andy Warhol, *Jean Vaughan (Golden shoe)*, 1956, gold leaf, ink, printed gold collage on paper, 41 x 28 cm. Venice, Luigino Rossi Collection.

117 Andy Warhol, *David Evins (Golden shoe)*, 1956, gold leaf, ink, printed gold collage on paper, 45.5 x 30.7 cm. Venice, Luigino Rossi Collection.

ROOM 5

118 Salvatore Ferragamo, *Zita*, 1925–30, court shoe in blue suede, 21.5 x 7 (heel height) cm. Florence, Salvatore Ferragamo Museum.

119 Salvatore Ferragamo, *Prototype for a court shoe*, 1929, patented calf upper covered with mechanised silk chain stitching embroidery, 21.5 x 7 (heel height) cm. Florence, Salvatore Ferragamo Museum.

120 Salvatore Ferragamo, *Two piece shoe*, 1932–35, raffia and kid upper, 23.5 x 4 (heel height) cm. Florence, Salvatore Ferragamo Museum.

121 Salvatore Ferragamo, *Prototype for a sandal*, 1935, red and white kid upper, 23.5 x 7.5 (heel height) cm. Florence, Salvatore Ferragamo Museum.

122 Salvatore Ferragamo, *Prototype for a laced shoe*, 1935, patchwork upper in black calf, *à jour* stitching in white kid, 21 x 7 (heel height) cm. Florence, Salvatore Ferragamo Museum.

123 Salvatore Ferragamo, *Laced shoe*, 1936–38, plaited bark and kid upper, 22.5 x 8.5 (heel height) cm. Florence, Salvatore Ferragamo Museum.

124 Salvatore Ferragamo, *Prototype for a sandal*, 1936–38, upper in hemp canvas embroidered in raffia with floral motif, 20 x 7 (heel height) cm. Florence, Salvatore Ferragamo Museum.

125 Salvatore Ferragamo, *Ninfea*, 1937, black antelope sandal, 24.5 x 8.5 (heel height) cm. Florence, Salvatore Ferragamo Museum.

126 Salvatore Ferragamo, *Spaghetti*, 1938, sandal in multicoloured suede, 22 x 8 (heel height) cm. Florence, Salvatore Ferragamo Museum.

127 Salvatore Ferragamo, *Sandal*, 1938, black satin upper, platform insole formed by four convex layers of cork covered with gold and silver calf, 25 x 6 (heel height) cm. Florence, Salvatore Ferragamo Museum.

128 Salvatore Ferragamo, *Sandal*, 1938, purple satin and gold kid upper, wedge heel formed with three cork layers covered with satin and kid, 23 x 3 (heel height) cm. Florence, Salvatore Ferragamo Museum.

129 Salvatore Ferragamo, *Two piece shoe*, 1938–39, patent kid upper, cork platform insole and wedge heel covered with kid, 23.5 x 8 (heel height) cm. Florence, Salvatore Ferragamo Museum.

130 Salvatore Ferragamo, *Ankle boot*, 1939, painted canvas, 22 x 9 (heel height) cm. Florence, Salvatore Ferragamo Museum.

131 Salvatore Ferragamo, *Unica*, 1939, copy of suede ankle boot, cork platform insole and wedge heel covered with suede, 23 x 9 (heel height) cm. Florence, Salvatore Ferragamo Museum.

132 Salvatore Ferragamo, *Mule*, 1939, red suede and gold kid upper, cork wedge heel covered with suede and kid, 23 x 6 (heel height) cm. Florence, Salvatore Ferragamo Museum.

133 Salvatore Ferragamo, *Sandal*, 1940, black satin upper, vertically fluted platform insole covered with golden kid, 20 x 6 (heel height) cm. Florence, Salvatore Ferragamo Museum.

134 Salvatore Ferragamo, *Diva*, 1941, sandal with multicoloured suede upper, cork wedge heel covered with suede, 23 x 8 (heel height) cm. Florence, Salvatore Ferragamo Museum.

135 Salvatore Ferragamo, *Closed shoe*, 1942, multicoloured patchwork suede upper, cork wedge heel covered with suede, 23 x 8 (heel height) cm. Florence, Salvatore Ferragamo Museum.

136 Salvatore Ferragamo, *Invisible*, 1947, sandal in lilac calf, vamp with nylon fishing threads, 23 x 8 (heel height) cm. Florence, Salvatore Ferragamo Museum.

137 Salvatore Ferragamo, *Sandal*, 1950, nylon mesh and golden kid upper, platform insole covered with kid, 24 x 10 (heel height) cm. Florence, Salvatore Ferragamo Museum.

138 Salvatore Ferragamo, *Damigella*, 1955, prototype for an ankle boot in elasticised golden silk brocade, 23 x 9 (heel height) cm. Florence, Salvatore Ferragamo Museum. The model was created for Sophia Loren.

139 Salvatore Ferragamo, *Court shoe*, 1959, golden kid upper, 24 x 11 (heel height) cm. Florence, Salvatore Ferragamo Museum. The model was worn by Marilyn Monroe in the *Bus Stop* film, directed by Joshua Logan.

140 Salvatore Ferragamo, *Court shoe*, 1959–60, upper covered with red rhinestones, 24 x 11 (heel height) cm. Florence, Salvatore Ferragamo Museum. The model was created for Marilyn Monroe in George Cukor's film *Let's Make Love* in 1960.

141 Salvatore Ferragamo, *Prototype for a mule*, 1960, multicoloured upper in calf, wood wedge heel covered with calf, 21 x 7.5 (heel height) cm. Florence, Salvatore Ferragamo Museum.

142 Stephen Jones, *Santa Banana*, from 'Tales of the Alhambra' Collection, Autumn-Winter 1984, jewelled plastic boater. London, Stephen Jones Millinery.

143 Stephen Jones, *Colorama*, from 'In Orbit' Collection, Autumn-Winter 1990, multicoloured felt roll cloche. London, Stephen Jones Millinery.

144 Stephen Jones, *Multi-coloured Butterfly of Love*, from 'Souvenirs' Collection, Spring-Summer 1993, tulle biba hat. London, Stephen Jones Millinery.

145 Stephen Jones, *Barneys*, from 'Xanadu' Collection, Autumn-Winter 1993, felt and rhinestone cloche. London, Stephen Jones Millinery.

146 Stephen Jones, *Rose Royce*, from 'Contours' Collection, Autumn-Winter 1996, velvet and satin top hat. London, Stephen Jones Millinery.

147 Stephen Jones, *Serengeti 1935*, from 'Murder by Millinery' Collection, Autumn-Winter 1997, stencilled felt paw hat. London, Stephen Jones Millinery.

148 Stephen Jones, *Vibe*, from 'E = mc²' Collection, Spring-Summer 1998, cane window hat. London, Stephen Jones Millinery.

149 Stephen Jones, *Cork Street*, from 'Millinery Computer' Collection, Autumn-Winter 1998, nylon flocked toque. London, Stephen Jones Millinery.

150 Stephen Jones, *Soho*, from 'Millinery Computer' Collection, Autumn-Winter 1998, metal trilby. London, Stephen Jones Millinery.

151 Stephen Jones, *Damn That Feels Good*, from 'Celebration!' Collection, Autumn-Winter 1999, wood multimedia turban. London, Stephen Jones Millinery.

152 Stephen Jones, *Witching Hour*, from 'Celebration!' Collection, Autumn-Winter 1999, jacquard clock hat. London, Stephen Jones Millinery.

153 Stephen Jones, *Tiki Lounge*, from 'Nursery' Collection, Spring-Summer 2000, Breton model in printed horsehair. London, Stephen Jones Millinery.

154 Stephen Jones, *AWOL*, from 'Blah Blah Blah' Collection, Autumn-Winter 2000, tulle silhouette top hat. London, Stephen Jones Millinery.

155 Stephen Jones, *Prequel*, from 'Blah Blah Blah' Collection, Autumn-Winter 2000, film strip and pleated silk cloche. London, Stephen Jones Millinery.

156 Stephen Jones, *Gruau*, from 'Blah Blah Blah' Collection, Autumn-Winter 2000, bidimensional wool crêpe cloche. London, Stephen Jones Millinery.

157 Stephen Jones, *Elena*, from 'Queens' Collection, Autumn-Winter 2001, leather sliced cap. London, Stephen Jones Millinery.

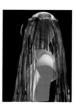

158 Stephen Jones, *Roxette*, from 'North' Collection, Autumn-Winter 2002, acetate ribbon headdress. London, Stephen Jones Millinery.

159 Stephen Jones, *SaamiAbbaGarbo*, from 'North' Collection, Autumn-Winter 2002, Hindi embroidered sequin and tulle cap. London, Stephen Jones Millinery.

160 Stephen Jones, *Tourist Trap*, from 'South' Collection, Spring-Summer 2003, multimedia sun hat. London, Stephen Jones Millinery.

161 Stephen Jones, *Niche*, from 'Hollywood Regency' Collection, Spring-Summer 2004, hand painted satin architectural cloche. London, Stephen Jones Millinery.

162 Stephen Jones, *Glorianna*, from 'Handmade in England' Collection, Spring-Summer 2005, muslin top hat. London, Stephen Jones Millinery.

163 Stephen Jones, *Ecstasy*, from 'Artifice' Collection, Spring-Summer 2007, photographic print of a mask. London, Stephen Jones Millinery.

164 Stephen Jones, *Ovation*, from 'Covent Garden' Collection, Autumn-Winter 2008, feather and jewel aigrette. London, Stephen Jones Millinery.

165 Stephen Jones, *XS*, from 'Covent Garden' Collection, Autumn-Winter 2008, embroidered velvet triangular beret. London, Stephen Jones Millinery.

166 Stephen Jones, *Coloratura*, from 'Covent Garden' Collection, Autumn-Winter 2008, operatic felt headdress. London, Stephen Jones Millinery.

167 Stephen Jones, *Folded Paper*, from 'Vanda' Collection, Spring-Summer 2009, origami paper flower, London, Stephen Jones Millinery.

168 Stephen Jones, *Loopy*, from 'Albertopolis' Collection, Autumn-Winter 2009, velvet and nylon fibre toque. London, Stephen Jones Millinery.

169 Stephen Jones, *À la carte*, from 'ABC' Collection, Spring-Summer 2010, satin and organza fascinator. London, Stephen Jones Millinery.

170 Stephen Jones, *Chic*, from 'ABC' Collection, Spring-Summer 2010, bugle bead beret. London, Stephen Jones Millinery.

171 Stephen Jones, *Je ne sais quoi*, from 'ABC' Collection, Spring-Summer 2010, straw and pink satin bicorne with rose. London. Stephen Jones Millinery.

ROOM 6

172 *Scarlet Macaw (Ara macao)*, naturalised specimen, 27 x 69 x 20 cm; 83 (total length) cm. Florence, Natural History Museum, 'La Specola' Zoology Section, Coll.Gen.Ucc. no.1146.

173 *White-eyed Parakeet (Aratinga leucophthalma)*, naturalised specimen, 25 x 23 x 15 cm; 41 (total length) cm. Florence, Natural History Museum, 'La Specola' Zoology Section, Coll.Gen.Ucc. no.1135.

174 Hellenistic Art, *Askos*, 3rd century BC, ceramic and black paint, 6 x 8 x 6 cm. Florence, National Archaeological Museum, Ancient Collections, inv. no. 4436.

175–176 Etruscan Art, *Little boot-shaped vases*, 8th century BC, ceramic from Poggio alla Guardia, Vetulonia (GR) and from Vetulonia (GR), 5,5 x 12 x 11; 6.5 x 11 x 17 cm. Florence, National Archaeological Museum, inv. nn. 8208; 6343.

177 Etruscan Art, *Crossed feet with sandals*, mid-2nd century BC, earthenware from temple in Catona (AR), 16.5 x 9.5 x 9 cm. Arezzo, 'Gaio Cilnio Mecenate' National Archaeological Museum, inv. no. 87694.

178 Etruscan Art, *Olla*, 7th century BC, ovoid olla in pasted ceramic painted with geometrical pattern from Poggio Buco (GR), 42 (diameter) x 40 cm. Florence, National Archaeological Museum, inv. no. 77127.

179 Roman Art, *Hemispheric bowl*, imperial age, 1st–2nd century AD, glass and mosaic. Florence, National Archaeological Museum, Ancient Collections, inv. no. 15920.

180 Roman Art, *Hemispheric bowl*, imperial age, 1st–2nd century AD, glass with green and blue stripes, 7.5 x 2.5 cm. Florence, National Archaeological Museum, Ancient Collections, inv. no. 15908.

181 Roman Art, *Hemispheric bowl*, imperial age, 1st–2nd century AD, glass with stripes in various colours, 10.5 x 6.5 cm. Florence, National Archaeological Museum, Ancient Collections, inv. no. 15905.

182 Roman Art, *Couple of foot with statue fit*, imperial age, 1st–3rd century AD, bronze, 8 x 16 x 21 cm. Florence, National Archaeological Museum, Ancient Collections, inv. nos. 1987-1988.

183 *Red legged Honeycreeper (Cyanerpes cyaneus)*, naturalised specimen, 13 x 19 x 6 cm; 13 (total length) cm. Florence, Natural History Museum, 'La Specola' Zoology Section, Coll.Gen.Ucc. no. 9535.

184 *Red tailed Comet (Sappho sparganura),* naturalised specimen, 10.5 x 26 x 12 cm; 16 (total length) cm. Florence, Natural History Museum, 'La Specola' Zoology Section, Coll.Gen. Ucc. no. 9540.

185 *Lovely Cotinga (Cotinga amabilis),* naturalised specimen, 21 x 23.5 x 7.5 cm; 23 (total length) cm. Florence, Natural History Museum, 'La Specola' Zoology Section, Coll.Gen.Ucc. no. 9537.

186 *Blue Dacnis (Dacnis cayana),* naturalised specimen, 11 x 19 x 9 cm; 11.5 (total length) cm. Florence, Natural History Museum, 'La Specola' Zoology Section, Coll.Gen.Ucc., no. 9536.

187 Salvatore Ferragamo, *Prototype for a sandal,* 1930, golden kid upper and brass pyramid heel, 23 x 6 (heel height) cm. Florence Salvatore Ferragamo Museum.

188 Salvatore Ferragamo, *Prototype for a sandal,* 1930, kid upper, 23 x 7.5 (heel height) cm. Florence, Salvatore Ferragamo Museum.

189 Salvatore Ferragamo, *Arcobaleno (Rainbow),* 1935, prototype for a court shoe in embroidered black suede, 24 x 9 (heel height) cm. Florence, Salvatore Ferragamo Museum.

190 Salvatore Ferragamo, *Laced shoe,*1938, antelope upper and heel height, toe in shape of a rhinoceros horn, 21.5 x 10 (heel height) cm. Florence, Salvatore Ferragamo Museum.

191 Salvatore Ferragamo, *Laced shoe,*1938, black antelope upper and wedge heel, toe in shape of a rhinoceros horn, 22 x 7 (heel height) cm. Florence, Salvatore Ferragamo Museum.

192 Salvatore Ferragamo, *Sandal,* 1938, golden kid upper, cork platform sole covered with painted satin in floral motifs, 22.5 x 8 (heel height) cm. Florence, Salvatore Ferragamo Museum.

193 Salvatore Ferragamo, *Sandal,* 1939–40, black velvet, silver and golden kid upper, wood high heel and 'flat through' sole covered with silver kid, cork platform insole covered with silver and golden kid, 24 x 13

(heel height) cm. Florence, Salvatore Ferragamo Museum.

194 Salvatore Ferragamo, *Sandal,* 1947, multicoloured patchwork suede upper, wood wedge heel covered with suede, 22 x 6 (heel height) cm. Florence, Salvatore Ferragamo Museum.

195. Salvatore Ferragamo, *Liu,* 1950, satin mule embroidered with floral motifs with internal cork wedge heel, 22 x 2 (heel height) cm. Florence, Salvatore Ferragamo Museum.

196 Salvatore Ferragamo, *Tibetia,* 1950, suede laced shoe with apron in crocheted string, cork wedge heel covered with suede, 22 x 3 (heel height) cm. Florence, Salvatore Ferragamo Museum.

197 Salvatore Ferragamo, *Pigmy,* 1950, suede laced shoe, cork wedge heel covered with brown suede, 22 x 3 (heel height) cm. Florence, Salvatore Ferragamo Museum.

198 Salvatore Ferragamo, *Ballerina,* 1953–57, beige and red kid upper, low leather heel, red opanke suede sole and back, 'Ballerina by Ferragamo' line, 23.5 x 0.5 (heel height) cm. Florence, Salvatore Ferragamo Museum.

199 Salvatore Ferragamo, *Ballerina,* 1953–57, yellow calf and red kid upper, low leather heel, red opanke suede sole and back, 'Ballerina by Ferragamo' line, 22.5 x 0.4 (heel height) cm. Florence, Salvatore Ferragamo Museum.

200 Salvatore Ferragamo, *Ballerina,* 1953–57, yellow kid and red suede upper, low leather heel, red opanke suede sole and back, 'Ballerina by Ferragamo' line, 21.5 x 0.5 (heel height) cm. Florence, Salvatore Ferragamo Museum.

201 Salvatore Ferragamo, *Ballerina,* 1953–57, white calf and brown suede upper, low leather heel, brown opanke suede sole and back, 'Ballerina by Ferragamo' line, 22.5 x 0.4 (heel height) cm. Florence, Salvatore Ferragamo Museum.

202 Salvatore Ferragamo, *Sandal,* 1955, multicoloured patchwork raffia upper, heel covered with red calf, 22 x 4.5 (heel height) cm. Florence, Salvatore Ferragamo Museum.

203 Salvatore Ferragamo, *Piumata,* 1956, prototype for a sandal with upper in yellow and light blue bird's feathers and golden kid, 23 x 7 (heel height) cm. Florence, Salvatore Ferragamo Museum.

204 Salvatore Ferragamo, *Sapo,* 1956–57, prototype for a sandal in silk, pink cellophane and grosgrain, 20 x 9 (heel height) cm. Florence, Salvatore Ferragamo Museum.

205 Salvatore Ferragamo, *Ima,* 1956–57, prototype for a soutache sandal with red and grey silk and satin upper, 21 x 9 (heel height) cm. Florence, Salvatore Ferragamo Museum.

206 Salvatore Ferragamo, *Variopinta,* 1957, prototype for a sandal, upper in white and brown bird's feathers and silver kid, 21.5 x 8 (heel height) cm. Florence, Salvatore Ferragamo Museum.

207 Salvatore Ferragamo, *Marika*, 1957, prototype for a sandal in red silk and grosgrain, 23 x 9 (heel height) cm. Florence, Salvatore Ferragamo Museum.

208 Salvatore Ferragamo, *Fiesta*, 1957, prototype for a sandal in golden kid decorated with Venetian glass beads, 21 x 9 (heel height) cm. Florence, Salvatore Ferragamo Museum.

209 Salvatore Ferragamo, *Selvaggia*, 1957, prototype for a court shoe in white satin with ornaments in black bird's feathers and rhinestones, 20 x 9 (heel height) cm. Florence, Salvatore Ferragamo Museum.

210 Salvatore Ferragamo, *Azzorre*, 1957, prototype for a court shoe with white satin upper embroidered with silver threads, decorations with pink silk butterflies and rhinestones, 23 x 8.5 (heel height) cm. Florence, Salvatore Ferragamo Museum.

211 Salvatore Ferragamo, *Ars*, 1957–60, prototype for high-heeled sandal in satin painted with bird of paradise motif, 23 x 7 (heel height) cm, Florence, Salvatore Ferragamo Museum.

212 Salvatore Ferragamo, *Court shoe*, 1958–59, golden kid upper, 23 x 10.5 (heel height) cm. Florence, Salvatore Ferragamo Museum.

213 Salvatore Ferragamo, *Filetia*, 1961, prototype for a court shoe in green satin with silver, rhinestones and bird's ornamental feathers, 21 x 9 (heel height) cm. Florence, Salvatore Ferragamo Museum.

214–218 Salvatore Ferragamo, *Jackie*, 1961, prototypes for a court shoe in red, light green, green and pink satin with silver, rhinestones and bird's feather ornaments, 21 x 8 (heel height) cm. Florence, Salvatore Ferragamo Museum.

219–221 Salvatore Ferragamo, *Chantal*, 1961, prototypes for a court shoe in brown and green satin with silver, rhinestones and bird's feather ornaments, 21 x 8 (heel height) cm. Florence, Salvatore Ferragamo Museum.

222 *Andean Cock of the rock (Rupicola peruviana)*, naturalised specimen, 27 x 31 x 9 cm; 35 (total length) cm. Florence, Natural History Museum, 'La Specola' Zoology Section, Coll.Gen.Ucc. no. 9539.

223 *European Roller (Coracias garrulus)*, naturalised specimen, 28 x 29 x 55 cm; 36 (total length) cm. Florence, Natural History Museum, 'La Specola' Zoology Section, Coll.Gen.Ucc. no. 9542.

224 *Asian Fairly-bluebird (Irena puella)*, naturalised specimen, 14 x 25 x 7 cm; 26 (total length) cm. Florence, Natural History Museum, 'La Specola' Zoology Section, Coll.Gen. Ucc. no. 9538.

225 *Red Lory (Eos bornea)*, naturalised specimen, 23 x 34 x 15 cm; 34 (total length) cm. Florence, Natural History Museum, 'La Specola' Zoology Section, Coll.Gen.Ucc. no. 1033.

226 Caucasian manufacture, *Men's shoes*, 19th century, upper in yellow leather stamped with a striped pattern, quarters and finishings in red leather, long and curved toe, 30 x 7.7 cm. Florence, Stibbert Museum, cat. no. 120; inv. no. 14.239.

227 Chamacoco manufacture (Gran Chaco, Bolivia), *White feathers diadem*, 19th century, feathers, plumes, vegetable fibres, 22 x 32 x 18 cm. Florence, Natural History Museum, Anthropology and Ethnology Section, inv. no. 7806.

228 Chamacoco manufacture (Gran Chaco, Bolivia), *Sceptre of white feathers*, 19th century, feathers, plumes, vegetable fibres, wood, rattlesnake's tail, 18 x 42 x 16 cm. Florence, Natural History Museum, Anthropology and Ethnology Section, inv. no. 21245.

229 Chamacoco manufacture (Gran Chaco, Bolivia), *Sceptre of white feathers*, 19th century, feathers, plumes, vegetable fibres, wood, rattlesnake's tail, 20 x 45 x 15 cm. Florence, Natural History Museum, Anthropology and Ethnology Section, inv. no. 21246.

230 Chinese manufacture, *Woman's jacket*, Ching dynasty, 19th century, embroidered black silk with a flounce and white silk collar and cuffs, Manchu style embroidered flowers, birds and butterflies, 166 x 104 cm. Florence, Stibbert Museum, inv. no. 7870.

231 Chinese manufacture, *Long-Pao*, Ching dynasty, 19th century, robe of a dignitary of the first rank made of silk embroidered with dragons, clouds and waves, high flounce embroidered with diagonal stripes, 148 x 106 cm. Florence, Stibbert Museum, inv. no. 7871.

232 Japanese manufacture, *Japanese armour, Akaito odoshi nimai-do tosei gusoku*, third quarter of the 16th century, the corset dates from a few years later; the rest of the suit is from the Edo period, 80 x 175 x 80 cm.

Florence, Stibbert Museum, inv. no. 7728. Armour of a high-ranking samurai of the Hosokawa clan, characterised by connections made of red silk tape. The helmet is signed by Myochin Fusamune.

233 Indian manufacture, *Maharata figure of bride*, 18th century, wedding dress composed of veil, tulle bodice with gold stitching, sash of tulle embroidered with flowers around the waist, red skirt with embroidered flounce and yellow trousers,

60 x 167 x 60 cm. Florence, Stibbert Museum, inv. no. 5857.

234 Italian manufacture, *Women's shoe (incomplete)*, around 1640, elongated toe, squared at the top, upper in white leather decorated with braids that form a zigzag pattern, 6.5 x 25 x 10 cm. Florence, Stibbert Museum, cat. no. 25, inv. no. 14.146.

235 Northern Italian manufacture, *Women's slippers*, second half of the 16th century, round-toed slippers with high arched wooden support, covered with brown leather and decorated with braids and fringes in red and ivory silk, 22 x from 14.5 to 19 (heel height) cm. Florence, Stibbert Museum, cat. no. 24, inv. no. 14.141.

236 Mundurucù manufacture (Brazil), *Headdress of red plumes*, 19th century, feathers, plumes, vegetable fibres, 28 x 45 x 19 cm; with base 32 x 50 x 32 cm. Florence, Natural History Museum, Anthropology and Ethnology Section, cat. no. 34.

237 Mundurucù manufacture (Brazil), *Sceptre of red feathers*, 19th century, feathers, plumes, vegetable fibres, wood, 13 x 71 x 13 cm. Florence, Natural History Museum, Anthropology and Ethnology Section, cat. no. 406.

238 Mundurucù manufacture (Brazil), *Sceptre of red feathers*, 19th century, feathers, plumes, vegetable fibres, wood, 13 x 72 x 13 cm. Florence, Natural History Museum, Anthropology and Ethnology Section, cat. no. 794.

239 Nez Perce manufacture (North America), *Pair of moccasins*, 1930, beaded upper, tanned skin with matching beaded leggings, 9.5 x 24.8 x 27.3 (height with leggings) cm. Toronto, The Bata Shoe Museum, cat. no. P81.0328A-D.

240 Saho manufacture (Eritrea), *Handbag in cotton canvas and glass beads*, 19th century, cotton canvas, shells and glass beads, 11 x 45 x 3 cm. Florence, Natural History Museum, Anthropology and Ethnology Section, cat. no. 13032.

241 Saho manufacture (Eritrea), *Handbag in leather and glass beads*, 19th century, leather, shells, glass beads, 15 x 45 x 4 cm. Florence, Natural History Museum, Anthropology and Ethnology Section, cat. no. 12590.

242 Sioux manufacture (North America), *Pair of moccasins*,1890, quelled and beaded moccasins in tanned skin, 10.9 x 27 x 11.5 cm. Toronto, The Bata Shoe Museum, cat. no. P81.0323.A.B.

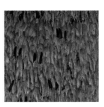

243 Tupinamba manufacture (Brazil), *Cloak of ibis rubra feathers*, 16th century, vegetable fibre, feathers, 170 x 125 x 8 cm. Florence, Natural History Museum, Anthropology and Ethnology Section, Medici Collections cat. no. 281.

244 *Olive Oropendola*, *(Psarocolius yuracares)*, naturalised specimen, 45 x 41 x 11 cm; 52 (total length) cm. Florence, Natural History Museum, 'La Specola' Zoology Section, Coll.Gen.Ucc. no. 9532.

245 *Guaiabero* *(Bolbopsittacus lunulatus)*, naturalised specimen, 11 x 25 x 6.5 cm; 19 (total length) cm. Florence, Natural History Museum, 'La Specola' Zoology Section, Coll.Gen.Ucc. no. 1111.

246 *Red-cheeked Parrot (Geoffroyus Geoffroyi)*, naturalised specimen, 29 x 29 x 10 cm; 39 (total length) cm, Florence, Natural History Museum, 'La Specola' Zoology Section, Coll.Gen.Ucc. no. 1080.

247 *Arfak Astrapia (Astrapia nigra)*, naturalised specimen, 75 x 44 x 19 cm; 75 (total length) cm. Florence, Natural History Museum, 'La Specola' Zoology Section, Coll.Gen.Ucc. no. 26.

248 *Raggiana Bird of Paradise (Paradisea raggiana)*, naturalised specimen, 44 x 49 x 46 cm; 38 (total length) cm. Florence, Natural History Museum, 'La Specola' Zoology Section, Coll.Gen. Ucc. no. 53.

249 *Superb Bird of Paradise (Lophorina superba)*, naturalised specimen, 22 x 30 x 24 cm; 28 (total length) cm. Florence, Natural History Museum, 'La Specola' Zoology Section, Coll.Gen. Ucc. no. 21.

250 *Mallee Ringnek (Barnardius barnardi)*, naturalised specimen, 29 x 29 x 20 cm; 39 (total lenght) cm. Florence, Natural History Museum, 'La Specola' Zoology Section, Coll.Gen.Ucc. no. 141.

251 *Eurasian Golden Oriole (Oriolus oriolus)*, naturalised specimen, 11 x 25 x 6.5 cm; 19 (total length) cm. Florence, Natural History Museum, 'La Specola' Zoology Section, Coll.Gen.Ucc. no. 9534.

252 *White Rhinoceros (Ceratotherium simum)*, complete mandible skull rhinoceros gathered in Congo Republic by Vittorio Emanuele Savoia Aosta, the count of Turin, in 1910, 71 x 69 x 30 cm. Florence, Natural History Museum, 'La Specola' Zoology Section, Coll.Gen. Mamm. no. 7529.

253 *Gorgeted Woodstar (Chaetocercus heliodor)*, naturalised specimen, 6 x 17 x 6 cm; 6 (total length) cm. Florence, Natural History Museum, 'La Specola' Zoology Section, Coll.Gen.Ucc. no. 9541.

254 *Brazilian Tanager (Ramphocelus bresilius)*, naturalised specimen, 16 x 23 x 6 cm; 20 (total length) cm. Florence, Natural History Museum, 'La Specola' Zoology Section, Coll.Gen.Ucc. no. 9533.

255 Lucio Venna, *Coturno Ferragamo*, 1930, advertising poster, chromo lithography on paper, 100 x 135 cm. Treviso, Museo Civico L. Bailo, Salce Collection.

BIBLIOGRAPHY

Arte moderna a Firenze, cataloghi di Esposizioni 1900-1933, edited by A. Calcagni Abrami, L. Chimirri (Florence: Centro Di, 1988).

G. Apollinaire, *La femme assise* (Paris: Éditions de la Nouvelle Revue Française, 1920).

G. Apollinaire, *Pittori cubisti. Meditazioni estetiche*, translated by F. Mimoia, with explanatory note by C. Carrà (Milan: SE Editore, 1996).

G. Balla, *Scritti futuristi*, comp. and edited by G. Lista (Milan: Abscondita, 2010).

G. Barche, 'Alfredo Bortoluzzi. "Al freddo" al Bauhaus', in *Bauhaus 1919-1933. Da Kandinsky a Klee, da Gropius a Mies van der Rohe* (Milan: Mazzotta, 1996).

C. Baudelaire, *Opere*, edited by G. Raboni, G. Montesano, introduction by G. Macchia (Milan: Mondadori, 1996).

A. Bonito Oliva, *Autocritico, automobile* (Rome: Castelvecchi, 2002).

I. Brin, *Usi e costumi 1920-1940* (Palermo: Sellerio, 1981).

I. Calvino, *Six Memos for the Next Millennium* (Harvard: Harvard University Press, 1988).

L. Cavalli Sforza, *L'evoluzione della cultura* (Turin: Codice Edizioni, 2004).

Creatività a colori / Creativity in Colour, exhibition catalogue (Florence, Salvatore Ferragamo Museum, December 6th 2006 – April 26th 2010), edited by S. Ricci (Livorno: Sillabe, 2006).

F. de Pisis, *Adamo o dell'eleganza. Per un'estetica del vestire*, edited by B. de Pisis, S. Zanotto (Milan: Abscondita, 2005).

S. Ferragamo, *Shoemaker of Dreams* (original edition London: George G. Harray & Co. Ltd, 1957, Livorno: Sillabe, 2006).

M. Fidolini, *Dal secondo futurismo al cartellone pubblicitario – Lucio Venna* (Bologna: Grafis Edizioni, 1987).

M. Fidolini, *Lucio Venna. Il siero futurista* (Pontedera: Bandecchi e Vivaldi, 1988).

H. Foster, R. Krauss *et alii*, *Arte dal 1900, Modernismo, Antimodernismo, Postmodernismo* (Bologna: Zanichelli, 2006).

Le futurisme à Paris, une avant-garde explosive, exhibition catalogue (Paris, Centre Georges Pompidou, October 15th 2008 – January 26th 2009), edited by D. Ottinger (Paris: Edition du Centre Georges Pompidou, 2008).

Il futurismo attraverso la Toscana, exhibition catalogue (Livorno, January 23rd – March 30th 2000), edited by E. Crispolti (Cinisello Balsamo: Silvana Editoriale, 2000).

Futurismo Moda Design, exhibition catalogue (Gorizia, Musei Provinciali, Borgo Castello, December 19th 2009 – May 1st 2010), edited by C. Cerutti, R. Sgubin (Gorizia: Musei Provinciali, 2009).

V. Gavioli, 'Balla. La vita e l'arte', in *Balla. I classici dell'arte* (Milan: Skira, 2004).

Greta Garbo. The Mystery of Style, exhibition catalogue (Milan, Triennale, February 28th – April 4th 2010; Florence, Salvatore Ferragamo Museum, May 13th – August 9th 2010), edited by S. Ricci (Milan: Skira, 2010).

R. Guénon, *Il Regno della Quantità e i Segni dei Tempi* (Milan: Adelphi, 1982).

R. Krauss, *Passaggi. Storia della scultura da Rodin alla Land Art* (Milan: Bruno Mondadori, 1998).

G. G. Lanza Del Vasto, *Pellegrinaggio alle sorgenti. Incontro con Gandhi e con l'India* (Milan: Il Saggiatore, 2005).

M. Leoni, G. Polizzi, 'Intervista a Gaspare Polizzi. Le attività 2008 della Biblioteca Filosofica,' in *Filosofia del Linguaggio: prospettiva di ricerca*, in 'Humana Mente' Il Pensiero della Biblioteca Filosofica Fiorentina, no. 4, February 2008.

G. Lista, *Balla* (Modena: Galleria Fonte d'Abisso, 1982).

G. Lista, *Futurismo. La rivolta dell'avanguardia / Die Revolte der Avantgarde* (Cinisello Balsamo: Silvana Editoriale, 2008).

R. Lunardi, 'La lavorazione della paglia,' in *Arti Fiorentine. La grande storia dell'Artigianato*, edited by R. Spinelli (Florence: Giunti, 2003), pp. 211–227.

A. Malochet, *Atelier Simultané di Sonia Delaunay 1923–1934* (Milan: Fabbri Editori, 1984).

G. Manzini, 'Tessili dell'avvenire. Sobrietà e eleganza,' in *La moda di Vanessa* (Palermo: Sellerio, 2003).

C. Morozzi, 'Progetti omeopatici,' in *The new Italian design – Il paesaggio mobile del nuovo design italiano*, exhibition catalogue (Milan, Triennale, January 20th – April 25th 2007), edited by S. Annicchiarico (Milan: Grafiche Milani, 2007), p. 6.

B. Munari, *Da cosa nasce cosa* (Bari: Laterza, 1981).

I Pittori Moderni della Realtà, edited by M. Fagiolo Dell'Arco (Florence: Vallecchi, 1984).

Platone, 'Menone,' in *Tutte le opere*, edited by G. Reale (Milan: Rusconi, 1997).

F. Ponzetta, *L'esoterismo nella cultura di destra. L'esoterismo nella cultura di sinistra* (Siena: Jubal, 2005).

G. Polizzi, 'Intervista a E. Garin,' in *Filosofia del linguaggio: prospettive di ricerca*, in 'Humana Mente,' Il Pensiero della Biblioteca Filosofica Fiorentina, no. 4, February 2008, p. 212.

E. Princi, 'Materiali futuristi,' in *Storia dell'Arte Universale*, vol. XVI, *Le Avanguardie* (Milan: Corriere della Sera Education, 2008).

P. Rabanne, *Trajectoire. D'une vie à l'autre* (Paris: France Loisirs, 1992).

S. Ricci, 'L'artigianato della moda,' in *Arti Fiorentine. La grande storia dell'Artigianato* (Florence: Giunti, 2003), pp. 229–256.

E. Schiaparelli, *Shocking Life* (London: Victoria and Albert Museum Ed., 2007).

M. Scudiero, *Depero Opere 1914–1953* (Milan-Cortina: Ed. Farsettiarte, 2008).

R. Sennett, *The Craftsman* (New Haven-London: Yale University Press, 2008).

G. Serafini, 'Un archetipo da inventare?,' in S. Mazza, *Scarperentola* (Milan: Idea Books, 1993), p. 17.

G. Severini, *Dal cubismo al classicismo. Estetica del numero e del compasso*, edited by E. Pontiggia (Milan: SE Editore, 1997).

Sonia Delaunay Atelier Simultané, exhibition catalogue (Bellinzona, April 12th – June 11th 2006), edited by A. Malochet, M. Bianchi (Milan: Skira, 2006).

Stephen Jones & The Accent of Fashion, exhibition catalogue (Antwerp, MoMu, Fashion Museum, September 8th 2010 – February 13th 2011), edited by G. Bruloot, K. Debo, in collaboration with S. Jones (Tielt, Belgium: Lannoo Publishers, 2010).

Storia della letteratura italiana, edited by E. Cecchi, N. Sapegno, vol. IX, *Il Novecento* (Milan: Garzanti, 1969).

A. M. Testa, *La trama lucente* (Milan: Rizzoli, 2010).

Thayaht. Vita, scritti, carteggi, edited by A. Scappini (Milan: Skira, 2005).

Thayaht. Un artista alle origini del Made in Italy, exhibition catalogue (Prato, Textile Museum, December 15th 2007 – April 14th 2008), edited by Prato Textile Museum (Prato: Museo del Tessuto Edizioni, 2007).

Various Authors, *Giovanni Costetti*, edited by R. Barilli and F. Ambrosetti, (Milan: Mazzotta, 1983).

Various Authors, *Leaders of Fashion. Salvatore Ferragamo (1898–1960)*, exhibition catalogue (Florence, Palazzo Strozzi, May 4th – June 30th 1985), edited by K. Aschengreen Piacenti, S. Ricci, G. Vergani (Florence: Centro Di, 1985).

Various Authors, *Thayaht. Futurista irregolare*, exhibition catalogue (Rovereto, Mart, June 11th – September 11th 2005), edited by D. Fonti (Milan: Skira, 2005).

E. Zolla, *Verità segrete esposte in evidenza. Sincretismo e fantasia. Contemplazione ed esotericità* (Venice: Marsilio, 1990).

E. Zolla, *Uscite dal mondo* (Milan: Adelphi, 1995).

Photographic References

Antonio Quattrone, Florence: pp. 11,
12, 13 (top), 14, 16 (top), 17, 18-19,
20, 21, 22, 23, 25, 28, 29, 30, 31, 32
(top), 33 (top), 34-35, 36, 37 (top),
38, 39 (top and in the middle), 41,
74, 81 (in the middle), 83, 84 (in the
middle), 87, 126, 143, 144, 145 (top
right and bottom left), 146, 147, 149,
150, 151 (top left and bottom right),
152 (top), 153.
Cecil B. DeMille Archive, Provo,
Brigham Young University: p. 48 (top).
Archivio Centrale dello Stato, Rome:
pp. 13 (in the middle), 68 (top), 93
(right), 105 (bottom left), 106 (top
right), 123 (bottom).
Historical Archive Data Bank Foto
Locchi, Florence: pp. 44, 45, 75, 114,
119 (top)
Historical Photographic Archives
of the Natural History Museum,
Anthropology and Ethnology Section,
Florence: p. 29 (left) (Guido Boggiani),
p. 24 (top) (Collezione Missione
Eritrea), p. 27 (F. A. Rinehart).
Bauhaus-Archiv, Berlin: p. 58 (bottom
right) (Walter Gropius).
Biagiotti Cigna Foundation, Rome:
pp. 58 (top), 86 (in the middle),
88-89, 103, 108 (top right).
Biblioteca Nazionale Centrale,
Florence: Cover, pp. 60, 61, 80, 93
(in the middle), 96, 100, 106, 110,
111 (right).
Bisazza: p. 134 (top).
CLM Seeber Collection, Rome:
p. 108.
Corbis: pp. 118 (David Lees),
51 (E.O. Hoppé), 79 (top right)
(Bettmann).
Diamantini & Domeniconi: p. 133
(left in the middle).
Droog Design: p. 133 (bottom right)
Farsettiarte, Prato: pp. 46, 57, 63, 92.
Getty Images - Hulton Archive: pp.
47 (bottom), 48 (bottom), 49, 79 (top
left and in the middle), 120 (top), 58
(bottom left) (Luigi Diaz), 50
(John Kobal Foundation), 78 (Hisham
Ibrahim), 47 (top) (Time and Life
Pictures).
Hamburger Kunsthalle, Hamburg:
p. 71 (top).
Librairie des Arts Décoratifs, Paris:
p. 85 (right).
MIBAC – Soprintendenza BSAE
per le province di Venezia, Belluno,
Padova e Treviso (by concession):
p. 52 (right).
Mobel Italia: p. 132 (top right).
Ugo Mulas Archive, Milan: p. 62.
Musée des Tissus de Lyon: pp. 59
(top left and bottom), 82, 85, 90 (left),
91 (in the middle), 92-93, 95 (top),
97 (top), 99, 101 (top), 104, 109 (top)
(Sylvain Pretto).

Musei Civici, Reggio Emilia: p. 120
(bottom left).
Musei Provinciali, Gorizia: pp. 102,
105.
Museo Richard-Ginori della
Manifattura di Doccia, Sesto Fiorentino,
Florence: p. 108 (bottom right).
Salvatore Ferragamo Museum,
Florence: pp. 52 (left), 79, 98 (top),
115, 116, 117, 132 (left in the middle
and bottom right); pp. 15 (bottom
left), 23 (bottom right), 25 (bottom
right), 26 (in the middle), 30 (in the
middle), 33 (bottom), 35 (bottom
right), 37 (bottom), 39 (bottom), 55
(top) 64, 69, 84 (top left), 87 (bottom),
88 (bottom), 102 (bottom) (Stefano
Biliotti); pp. 13 (bottom right), 15 (top
left), 16 (bottom), 19 (bottom right),
20 (bottom left), 24 (bottom), 40, 66,
68 (bottom), 70, 81 (top and bottom),
82 (bottom right), 85 (in the middle),
90 (bottom), 91 (top left and bottom
right), 95 (bottom), 98 (bottom), 101
(bottom), 125, 127, 132 (top left,
in the middle right and bottom left),
142 (bottom), 145 (bottom right),
146 (bottom left), 148 (bottom left),
150 (bottom left), 152 (bottom left)
(Christopher Broadbent); pp. 26
(top), 28 (bottom left), 32 (bottom),
71 (bottom), 82 (bottom left), pp. 84
(bottom), 86 (left), 97 (bottom), 105
(bottom right), 107 (bottom), 109 (in
the middle), 111 (bottom left), 119
(bottom), 133 (top left, right in the
middle and bottom left), 134 (bottom)
(Roberto Quagli).
Private Collection, Florence: pp. 55
(bottom), 73.
Private Collection, Pistoia: p. 120
(bottom right).
Private Collection, Rome: p. 107 (top).
Private Collection, Luigino Rossi,
Venice: p. 65.
Private Collection, Ottavio and Rosita
Missoni, Milan: p. 89 (right).
Sandro Michahelles Fotografo,
Florence: pp. 53, 54, 104 (in the
middle), 121, 122.
Stephen Jones Millinery, London: pp.
138, 139, 140, 141, 142, 145 (top
left), 148, 151 (top right and bottom
left), 152 (bottom right).
P. Salvini, Florence: p. 123 (top).
The Bata Shoe Museum, Toronto,
Canada: pp. 26 (bottom), 27 (bottom).
Tornabuoni Arte, Florence: p. 67
Vitra: p. 133 (top right).
Wolfgang Woessner, Vienna: p. 59
(top right).

The Salvatore Ferragamo Museum
is at the disposal of the entitled
parties as regards all unidentified
iconographic sources.